S. Hrg. 114–518

MILLENNIUM CHALLENGE CORPORATION: LESSONS LEARNED AFTER A DECADE AND OUTLOOK FOR THE FUTURE

HEARING

BEFORE THE

COMMITTEE ON FOREIGN RELATIONS UNITED STATES SENATE

ONE HUNDRED FOURTEENTH CONGRESS

FIRST SESSION

DECEMBER 8, 2015

Printed for the use of the Committee on Foreign Relations

(

Available via the World Wide Web: http://www.gpo.gov/fdsys/

U.S. GOVERNMENT PUBLISHING OFFICE

22–414 PDF WASHINGTON : 2016

For sale by the Superintendent of Documents, U.S. Government Publishing Office
Internet: bookstore.gpo.gov   Phone: toll free (866) 512–1800; DC area (202) 512–1800
Fax: (202) 512–2104   Mail: Stop IDCC, Washington, DC 20402–0001

COMMITTEE ON FOREIGN RELATIONS

BOB CORKER, TENNESSEE, *Chairman*

JAMES E. RISCH, Idaho	BENJAMIN L. CARDIN, Maryland
MARCO RUBIO, Florida	BARBARA BOXER, California
RON JOHNSON, Wisconsin	ROBERT MENENDEZ, New Jersey
JEFF FLAKE, Arizona	JEANNE SHAHEEN, New Hampshire
CORY GARDNER, Colorado	CHRISTOPHER A. COONS, Delaware
DAVID PERDUE, Georgia	TOM UDALL, New Mexico
JOHNNY ISAKSON, Georgia	CHRISTOPHER MURPHY, Connecticut
RAND PAUL, Kentucky	TIM KAINE, Virginia
JOHN BARRASSO, Wyoming	EDWARD J. MARKEY, Massachusetts

LESTER E. MUNSON III, *Staff Director*
JODI B. HERMAN, *Democratic Staff Director*

CHRIS FORD, *Majority Chief Counsel*
MARGARET TAYLOR, *Minority Chief Counsel*
JOHN DUTTON, *Chief Clerk*

(II)

CONTENTS

MILLENNIUM CHALLENGE CORPORATION: LESSONS LEARNED AFTER A DECADE AND OUTLOOK FOR THE FUTURE

TUESDAY, DECEMBER 8, 2015

U.S. SENATE,
COMMITTEE ON FOREIGN RELATIONS,
Washington, DC.

The committee met, pursuant to notice, at 10:14 a.m., in room SD–419, Dirksen Senate Office Building, Hon. Bob Corker (chairman of the committee) presiding.

Present: Senators Corker, Johnson, Flake, Gardner, Perdue, Cardin, Menendez, Shaheen, Coons, Murphy, Kaine, and Markey.

OPENING STATEMENT OF HON. BOB CORKER, U.S. SENATOR FROM TENNESSEE

The CHAIRMAN. Now the hearing for the Senate Foreign Relations Committee will come to order. Before we start, I want to say that today's hearing, by the way, in large part is due to some things that Senator Cardin would like to look at, and I appreciate his interest. Today's hearing will review the current operations and authority of the Millennium Challenge Corporation. The MCC, created a decade ago, was intended to take a unique approach to the development and foreign aid.

As designed, the MCC provides development assistance for clearly defined economic objectives in full partnership with a developing country. MCC compacts are earned, not given. With a set of clear indicators that emphasize democratic governance and economic freedoms that determine selectivity, the MCC works with successful countries committed to establishing appropriate enabling environments in which entrepreneurship and economic growth can thrive.

Further, MCC is unique in that this process is strongly driven by data and transparency. Today we will examine how MCC is fulfilling its original promise as an independent aid agency committed to identifying and removing constraints to economic growth working in full partnership with the host country. It is my hope we can discuss both the lessons learned along the way, but also ways we can help improve the MCC model.

And I want to turn to Senator Cardin for his comments.

OPENING STATEMENT OF HON. BENJAMIN L. CARDIN, U.S. SENATOR FROM MARYLAND

Senator CARDIN. Well, Mr. Chairman, again, let me thank you for bringing forward this hearing on the Millennium Challenge Corporation. I think my colleagues are aware that this program was established in 2004. It was unique in that it built upon U.S. ideals of entrepreneurship and good governance in order to do major infrastructure in a country, pretty much directed by that country. But they need to be able to establish that they are, in fact, governed by democratic goals, that they have economic freedom, and they invest in their own people.

So it is basically our values directed by their priorities that leverage a great deal of investment with strong accountability. And it has worked extremely well during this period of time, and I think by all accounts it has been given a very high grade for developing the type of economic growth in these countries that will sustain our values.

What I had asked the chairman, along with Senator Flake, is why should we not be looking at regional issues when we look at the countries that are involved; when you deal with trade, or you deal with transportation, you deal with energy. It does not end at one border. And why should we not be able to use the same principles to do regional grants?

And that legislation was filed. It does present certain challenges on accountability. It is different than how is it working within this model. So I hope during the course of this hearing we will have a chance to explore that expansion of authority and whether it would further advance the goals of a very successful program.

I welcome our witnesses, and I look forward to the hearing.

The CHAIRMAN. Thank you. Our first witness for the first panel is the Honorable Dana Hyde, chief executive officer of the Millennium Challenge Corporation. We want to thank you for being here. I know you know well about how we receive testimony. If you would summarize in about five minutes, we will, without objection, take your full written statement as part of the record.

If you would begin. Again, we thank you for your work and your willingness to be here today.

STATEMENT OF HON. DANA J. HYDE, CHIEF EXECUTIVE OFFICER, MILLENNIUM CHALLENGE CORPORATION, WASHINGTON, DC

Ms. HYDE. Thank you. Thank you, Chairman Corker, Ranking Member Cardin, and members of the committee. I am delighted to be here this morning and to have the opportunity to discuss the Millennium Challenge Corporation's work and our proposal to scale our investments through regional work.

Just over a decade ago, the Bush administration and Congress worked together to create an agency with just one focus: reducing poverty through economic growth. Now, this new agency was built on the lessons of decades of development, and it was charged with strengthening the U.S. effort to lift people out of poverty. Today, what started as a grand experiment is now an established and respected tool of U.S. international development.

You do have my testimony, Mr. Chairman, and that details MCC's unique model and accomplishments. So this morning I would like to focus on just two areas. First, how MCC is catalyzing change and growth around the world, and second, how MCC can maximize our impact through regional investments.

Simply stated, MCC is working to reduce poverty in three ways: first, by incentivizing countries to make meaningful reforms, second, by funding projects with tangible outcomes and real impact, and third, by focusing on systemic change that will outlive MCC's engagement.

As you know, countries must pass a scorecard to become eligible for compact assistance. This scorecard, an independent assessment of 20 key indicators, has proven to be a powerful incentive for countries to strengthen their democracies. Cote d'Ivoire is a prime example. Several years ago they set out to pass the scorecard. At the time they were failing 15 of the 20 indicators, including corruption. They established a special team within the prime minister's of- fice that changed the laws, including providing rights to women and tighten controls on corruption. If you were traveling in Abidjan in 2013, you would have seen billboards across the city with warn- ings to officials and citizens about the consequences of corruption. These efforts paid off. In 2016, Cote d'Ivoire passes 13 of 20 indi- cators and is a candidate for selection for an MCC compact. Cote d'Ivoire illustrates how MCC's competitive approach incentivizes reform before a dollar of taxpayer money is spent. At the same time, projects themselves must be targeted to achieve real out- comes.

I recently returned from Jordan, one of the most water scarce countries in the world. There, MCC supported a public-private partnership to finance the expansion of the country's primary wastewater treatment plant. This PPP, one of the first in the coun- try, leveraged $110 million, surpassing MCC's own $93 million in- vestment. The compact is being completed under time, under budg- et, and is expected to benefit nearly three million Jordanians. By crowding in private investment, MCC is multiplying its impact many times over.

The same is true in Ghana. In many ways, Ghana represents the evolution of an opportunity for MCC's work. In the first compact, MCC worked in many areas: road, agriculture, and water. MCC's second compact is solely focused on energy, and leveraging our credibility to support politically difficult reforms that will unlock barriers to private investment. In fact, MCC's reforms are already helping to catalyze more than $4 billion in private investment in Ghana's power sector, including General Electric's investment in a $1.8 billion power project.

In these ways, MCC's compacts leave behind more than the sum of the project, and we continue to pursue opportunities to increase leverage. In today's interconnected world, we believe regional in- vestments in sectors like transportation or power represent that opportunity.

In West Africa, for example, coordinating or pooling national grids is essential to increasing access to electricity. With the re- gional investment, MCC could concentrate our effort not just on one country like Ghana, but on the hard and soft infrastructure necessary better to integrate power grids across borders.

This summer, I was privileged to join some of the members of this committee at the AGOA conference in Gabon. Among the African delegates, the widespread view was that over the next decade, regional integration will be a primary driver of economic growth on the continent. MCC risks missing opportunities and leaving development impact on the table if it focuses solely on engagements that stop at borders.

With your support, regional investments can help turn the frontier markets of today into the emerging market partners of tomorrow. I am deeply grateful to Senators Cardin, Flake, Coons, and Isakson for introducing legislation that would give MCC this authority.

Mr. Chairman, as I conclude, let me emphasize what you noted earlier this year when you said "With limited aid dollars, it is—it is our responsibility to ensure American resources are used in the most effective manner possible." I can assure you the 300 professionals at MCC think about that responsibility every day. MCC is a lean and efficient agency that punches far above its weight. In little over a decade, it has helped foster growth and promote American values around the world. And since day one, MCC has held itself accountable to Congress and to the American people.

I want to thank you again for your time and your support of MCC's mission, and I would be delighted to answer your questions.

[The prepared statement of Ms. Hyde follows:]

PREPARED STATEMENT OF DANA J. HYDE

Thank you Chairman Corker, Ranking Member Cardin and members of the Senate Foreign Relations Committee for the opportunity to discuss the Millennium Challenge Corporation's (MCC) work to fight poverty, and the increased impact MCC can have through regional investments.

Just over a decade ago, the previous administration and Congress worked together to create an agency with a singular focus: reducing poverty through economic growth. This new agency, built on the lessons of 50 years of development assistance, faced many questions and an uncertain future:

- Could the United States use an evidence-based approach to select relatively well-governed countries and effectively and transparently fight poverty?
- Could poor countries make data-driven investment decisions and implement large projects within 5 years and without corruption?
- Could an innovative agency with a singular mission serve to promote American values—open markets, democracy, and good governance—while helping to support security and stability in poor countries around the globe?

Over the past decade, each of these questions has been answered in the affirmative. What started as a grand experiment is today an established and respected tool of U.S. development and economic engagement around the globe. MCC has become a key driver of good governance standards in poor countries, while simultaneously rising through the ranks to be recognized as one of the most transparent development agencies in the world.

MCC's country-led and country-owned implementation model has successfully delivered hundreds of projects that are improving the lives of an estimated 175 million people around the world. In an increasingly globalized economy, these investments are a down payment on stability and market opportunities for American businesses. MCC's engagement with a partner often stands as the cornerstone of the U.S. economic relationship in that country—visible proof that U.S. economic assistance leads to tangible results—and helps to create a more attractive environment for private investment.

THE MCC MODEL & PORTFOLIO

Over the span of its first decade, MCC committed roughly $10 billion to programs, signing compacts with 25 countries. About 65 percent of the compact portfolio was invested in Africa, with the rest in Central America, Eastern Europe, the Middle East, and Asia.

Overall, approximately 70 percent of MCC's portfolio has been invested in infra-structure—power, roads, ports, and bridges—that connects people to jobs, markets and opportunities. With large-scale grants that average $350 million and a 5-year time horizon, MCC is uniquely suited to tackle projects of this size and complexity. And while much of MCC's early infrastructure investments were focused on roads and transportation, the portfolio is increasingly invested in energy infrastructure; four of the last five compacts considered by MCC's Board—Ghana, Benin, Liberia and Tanzania—are aimed at helping create the conditions for private investment in energy in Africa.

MCC was founded on the principle of data-driven and evidence-based decision-making, which permeates every aspect of our work. It starts with economists from MCC and an eligible country jointly conducting an upfront analysis to determine the country's binding constraints to economic growth. Based upon this analysis, con-cepts, sectors, and ultimately projects are identified and assessed for potential impact and cost effectiveness. MCC is looking to fund projects with at least a 10 percent economic rate of return (ERR) over a 20-year period. In fact, what we have seen—in a sampling of projects recently completed—is that the average ERR upon completion is actually over 16 percent.

Once a compact is shaped and signed, MCC monitors implementation progress, including through quarterly reviews. MCC tracks contracts signed and funds spent, outputs achieved, any outcomes that can be determined during the course of a project, and whether our partner countries are implementing the agreed-upon policy reforms. We disburse funds quarterly if the benchmarks are being met. We will withhold funds—and may even cut off assistance—if the conditions no longer meet MCC standards. In addition, MCC seeks an independent evaluation of every project, with gold standard performance and impact evaluations conducted by universities, researchers and other outside experts.

Finally, MCC's model is unique because of our size and footprint. MCC has just over 300 full-time employees, and our overseas presence is only about one or two Americans in each country. Despite being so lean, MCC is able to effectively and efficiently disburse about 1 billion dollars per year in grant investments because we require the host government to implement the compact—with strong MCC oversight and monitoring—through an independent entity the government creates, often called the Millennium Challenge Account (MCA).

A FOCUS ON MEASURABLE RESULTS

A commitment to achieving and measuring results is at the core of MCC's model. MCC looks at results in the following three ways: (1) the reforms MCC incentivizes countries to make; (2) the outcomes and impact of the projects MCC funds; and (3) the ways in which MCC fosters self-sufficiency in partner countries.

First, MCC achieves some of its most dramatic results without spending a dime of taxpayer resources. MCC's stringent eligibility criteria and its global credibility have created a powerful incentive for reform, dubbed the MCC Effect. Countries are changing their laws in order to improve their performance on MCC's annual score-cards and qualify for MCC assistance. Indeed, researchers at the College of William and Mary have carefully studied and documented this effect, finding that MCC's scorecard is one of the most influential external tools to incentivize policy reform.[1] Cote d'Ivoire provides a striking example. For several years, a special team within the Prime Minister's office has worked across government ministries to address scorecard concerns ranging from health to women's empowerment to the business environment to corruption. In 2013, Cote d'Ivoire passed only 5 of 20 indicators on its MCC scorecard. Fast forward just three years and Cote d'Ivoire now passes 13 of 20 indicators—and is a candidate for selection for an MCC compact.

Moreover, the incentive effect does not end once a country is selected as a partner. MCC continues to monitor governance performance throughout the partnership while using its hard-earned credibility to push for major policy and sectoral reforms that complement and sustain the project investments. Together, these reforms and

---

[1] Parks, Bradley C., and Zachary J. Rice. " Measuring the Policy Influence of the Millennium Challenge Corporation: A Survey-Based Approach." The College of William and Mary, February 2013.

investments help to crowd in private sector investment and create opportunities for more growth.

Second, MCC's projects—in and of themselves—are designed to reduce poverty and create growth. In little over a decade, MCC has already had a lasting impact on countries, communities, and individuals around the world. From a road in the Philippines strong enough to withstand Typhoon Haiyan and facilitate rescue efforts to a port expansion in Benin that resulted in a 75 percent increase in cargo, MCC has shown a country-driven model of development can work, and work well. As a result of MCC's work:

- Millions of people will travel over more than 2,850 kilometers of roads, connecting businesses to markets and fueling domestic and international trade;
- Millions more will be able to light their homes and start new businesses thanks to 4,400 kilometers of new energy transmission lines and the sector reforms that MCC has required to promote private investment
- 300,000 households have legal rights to their lands, empowering women as heads of households, increasing individual access to credit, and reducing land-related conflicts;
- 680,000 people have access to clean water, unleashing economic growth potential by, among other things, improving health and life expectancy; and
- 215,000 students have access to schools, including girls in Burkina Faso whose improved math and French test scores will mean greater opportunities to enter and be successful in the labor market.

Finally, MCC's compacts leave behind more than the sum of their individual projects. MCC's focus is not just on building infrastructure, but on building expertise and know-how.

This is evident in Honduras, which has adopted standards of transparency and accountability put in place by MCC to implement additional projects even after MCC's compact had closed. In Cabo Verde, the Government passed a new law on public procurement based on MCC's procurement guidelines. And in Senegal, MCC worked to improve local land governance through a blend of traditional and modern land practices, an approach now being widely adopted by the Government of Senegal.

Through MCC's unique country-led approach, countries learn successful project implementation, accountable fiscal stewardship, and transparent procurement processes that outlast the lifetime of a compact. When combined, MCC's abilities to incentivize reforms, drive results, and build self-sufficiency enable the agency to punch above its weight and deliver outsized impact.

LEVERAGING THE PRIVATE SECTOR

In today's development landscape, traditional aid dynamics are changing. The private sector plays an increasingly vital role in delivering public goods. In sub-Saharan Africa, Official Development Assistance (ODA) comprised 62 percent of external flows in 1990; by 2012, ODA was just 22 percent of external flows to Africa.[2] Total foreign investment to sub-Saharan Africa rose from just $1.7 billion in 1990 to a record high of $42.2 billion last year. These resources are more critical than ever in addressing development needs.

This is why everything about MCC's model and approach—from selecting countries to developing compacts, from fighting corruption to measuring results—is oriented around creating the right circumstances for businesses to invest. Simply stated, catalyzing the private sector for development is foundational to MCC's work and helps ensure the long-term sustainability of our investments.

As part of this commitment, MCC is increasingly adopting innovative approaches to specifically integrate the private sector into our compacts. MCC helps countries design and implement public-private partnerships; utilizes creative grant facilities to draw out innovation from the private sector; provides viability gap financing to allow projects to reach successful financial close; and targets policy reforms that open up private sector market opportunities. The agency is also bolstering efforts to engage American companies on business opportunities through investment summits here in the United States and trade missions abroad.

These practices enable MCC to leverage America's investments and multiply its impact. To illustrate, in three recent compacts—Benin, Ghana and Jordan—MCC's total investment of $1.1 billion is helping to mobilize nearly $5 billion in private investment.

---

[2] Sy, Amadou. "Private Capital Flows, Official Development Assistance, And Remittances to Africa: Who Gets What?" The Brookings Institution, May 2015.

For instance, I was recently in Jordan to inaugurate the expansion of the As-Samra Wastewater Treatment Plant. Building on USAID's previous work, MCC utilized a public-private partnership to support upgrades to the country's wastewater network system, mobilizing an additional $110 million in private financing. As-Samra will address 70 percent of Jordan's wastewater treatment needs, and thanks to private sector investments in cutting-edge efficient and environmentally sound engineering designs, the plant will self-produce more than 75 percent of the energy required for its operations through clean biogas and hydropower. The deal's financing structure, a build-operate-transfer agreement, provides for high quality operation and maintenance by the private sector operator for the next 22 years, fur- ther ensuring the sustainability of the U.S. taxpayers' investment. The facility, com- bined with MCC's other projects in Jordan, is expected to benefit approximately 3 million people.

Shifting to Ghana, MCC's $500 million investment focuses on turning around the country's main utility by funding the public infrastructure and sectoral reforms that are necessary to make private sector-financed power generation projects financially viable. As a result of the compact's reforms and investments, over $4 billion in private investments in the Ghanaian power sector is expected in coming years, including $1 billion from General Electric.

Furthermore, MCC invested almost $190 million to double the capacity of Benin's national port, which contributes nearly two-thirds of tax revenue and impacts one-quarter of the nation's GDP. Through a global competition, Benin selected a private investor and operator, which invested an additional $256 million in customized improvements, bringing greater volumes, efficiencies and revenues, and winning a top global prize as an innovative private-public partnership.

TRANSPARENCY & ACCOUNTABILITY

MCC is clear about what the agency aims to achieve and holds itself accountable for reaching its goals. MCC tracks and measures results meticulously and transparently to ensure that its programs are effective and efficient, thus maximizing valuable taxpayer resources. MCC holds itself accountable, as it does its partner countries, and will continue to learn, share, and adapt based on the results it measures.

The data we track provides valuable insights into what is working and what is not, including instances where MCC programs met or exceeded output targets but the subsequent evaluations did not find attributable impact on incomes. In addition to the internal learning this data provides, MCC also contributes to the wider body of knowledge on many of the assumptions underpinning methods of delivering foreign assistance.

Building on a legacy of transparency, and the advice of this Committee, MCC is producing "after action reports" for completed compacts to make the collected data more comprehensive and accessible. I look forward to continuing our work with you to find ways to better capture and share MCC's robust data, monitoring and evaluation systems. This Committee has recently shown its support for the increased use of metrics, monitoring and evaluation, and transparency that are the hallmarks of MCC by approving the Foreign Aid Transparency and Accountability Act, which supports high standards of data transparency and accountability.

GROWTH, TRADE & REGIONAL INTEGRATION

In today's global economy, growth is more dependent than ever on trade and regional integration. Regional integration has been a proven accelerator of growth and poverty reduction in places like East Asia. Poor countries grow faster, create more jobs, and attract more investment when they are part of dynamic regional markets.

As a development agency solely committed to fighting poverty through economic growth, MCC risks leaving development impact and investment returns on the table if it solely focuses on engagements that stop at the border. Investing in the context of larger markets will allow MCC to capture greater economies of scale and raise returns in relation to costs.

MCC is well positioned to invest regionally for the benefit of poor countries, in Africa, South Asia, and Central America. MCC has the technical capacity and a successful track record of delivering large, complex infrastructure projects, and can deploy that capacity for cross-border investments. Just as important, MCC has experience incentivizing and supporting difficult policy and institutional reforms. That work can and should now be extended to a multi-country context. Bringing together both the hardware and the software of regional integration will be essential to make dynamic regional markets work.

The challenges of multi-country investments should not be underestimated. But MCC has already begun devising solutions to those new challenges. Given the potential rewards, the risks of inaction are also significant. By making coordinated regional investments across multiple eligible countries, MCC can help countries work together to build and grow regional markets; expand and link regional power, transport, and water networks to reduce costs and improve service; capture more benefits through economies of scale; facilitate increased trade and investment; and help generate new business and market opportunities for U.S. and other companies. Regional investments can help translate the frontier markets of today into tomorrow's emerging market partners of the U.S.

That is why MCC is seeking to work regionally with partners when the economic analysis calls for it, consistent with the foundational principle of country-led accountability. Additionally, allowing for regional MCC investments would be a significant tool for the U.S. to increase trade capacity and improve the uptake of AGOA preferences for eligible countries.[3] This is one of the reasons the House Foreign Affairs Committee has approved language to facilitate MCC's regional work in bipartisan legislation, H.R. 2845, the AGOA Enhancement Act of 2015. I am deeply grateful to Sens. Cardin, Flake, Coons, and Isakson for championing Senate legislation, S. 1605, that would also give MCC this authority.

As you have noted in the Global Gateways Trade Capacity Act, Mr. Chairman, stable trading relationships promote security and prosperity, and can foster the expansion of open markets and democracy. Aid to developing countries for trade capacity building can have other positive side effects such as promoting best practices, encouraging good governance, combating corruption, and reforming legal regimes.

By giving MCC the authority it needs to make regional investments, this Committee can take a critical step toward reducing global poverty.

CONCLUSION

The development community faces many questions and challenges as the face of global poverty changes. Among other things, MCC, with your support, needs to think hard about how best to measure poverty in potential partner countries.

But we also know that, in the interwoven world of the 21st century, investment in effective development, alongside defense and diplomacy, promotes shared security and shared prosperity.

I want to echo your statement earlier this year, Mr. Chairman, when you said that "with limited aid [dollars] available, it is our responsibility to ensure American resources are used in the most effective manner possible."

I am proud to lead an agency built on the pillars of effective development. And I believe that MCC is uniquely positioned to contribute in the current global context and in the current budget climate. MCC's catalytic investments yield results in their own right while supporting the policies and good governance that will allow developing countries to reduce poverty by growing their own economies.

The challenge is great. More than half of MCC's current partners have more than half of their population living on less than $2 a day. These are among the poorest countries in the world, and MCC works with them because they pass a high bar for their commitment to sound economic and social policies that will reduce poverty among their own citizens. MCC incentivizes this commitment through our competitive standards. We accelerate this commitment through high-value investments in economic growth. And we seek to embed in our partner countries a culture of accountability, transparency, and responsible stewardship that help sustain and scale progress.

MCC also has a critical role as a soft power tool that advances U.S. values and builds a more secure and prosperous future. Today, MCC is the single most important bilateral channel for U.S. aid in support of economic growth—the strongest driver of sustained poverty reduction—and its investments help channel U.S. assistance to the best governed poor countries. MCC helps drive U.S. efforts to promote American values and the market democracy model. And MCC is creating new opportunities for the private sector, including U.S. businesses, to invest and grow.

Through their support for MCC, the American people are helping create the building blocks of growing economies and stronger societies around the world. This means better governance, less poverty and more economic opportunity; vital elements of peace and stability in their countries and in ours.

Thank you very much for your time and attention.

---

[3] Government Accountability Office." African Growth and Opportunity Act: USAID Could Enhance Utilization by Working with More Countries to Develop Export Strategies" January 2015.

The CHAIRMAN. Well, again, thank you for being here, and I do want to thank Senator Flake, Senator Isakson, Senator Cardin, and Senator Coons for looking at creative ways to cause MCC to have greater impact.

Ms. Hyde, you and I have met in the office, and I understand the purpose of MCC was to be transformative. I told you about one of my first trips to Mali where I saw people in extreme poverty, if you will, people transporting goods on their head down the street and—

Ms. HYDE. Yes.

The CHAIRMAN [continuing]. On donkeys and other kinds of manual transportation. And yet we were building this massive airport there, and how, candidly, I was having some difficulties connecting the two in terms of level of economic development. I wonder if you might explain to others here your thinking on this, and how your thinking may have evolved since our meeting.

Ms. HYDE. Thank you. I appreciate the question, Mr. Chairman. MCC's thinking has evolved in a number of important ways. I would say that the principles that MCC was founded on, that countries themselves have to be full partners in the development effort in order for it to be sustainable, and how that relates to our actual work in project selection, and then how we evaluate projects, is certainly one of the lessons that we have learned.

So, for example, I believe at the time of the Mali compact, which was one of our first compacts, I think it was shaped in year three of what was a startup agency at the time. At the time, we did not have in place an economic analytic tool called the constraints-to-growth analysis, which is the way we now engage with countries to say what are the binding constraints-to-growth in this economy and how do we go from the 30,000 foot level down to a project level. We also put in place a cost-benefit analysis to do an Economic Rate of Return (ERR) for every project that we do and we are looking to achieve a 10 percent ERR.

These are both lessons that we learned over the years and that we believe put more rigor and accountability around our projects. So I would say those are two things in place that were not in place at the time of the Mali compact.

Now, at the end of that compact, as you know, there was a coup in Mali, and MCC actually terminated its compact because of the accountability framework we work in, meaning you have to maintain the governance standards throughout the life of our compact.

The CHAIRMAN. So whatever happened to the airport?

Ms. HYDE. The airport itself was not completed by MCC. I believe it was Mali's funds with another donor that came in to finance it. There was also some question, just a factual question, Mr. Chairman, about what you saw. Our work was mostly around the runway, rehabilitation and the renovation of one of the terminals, so I am not actually clear what it was you saw.

The CHAIRMAN. So, that is interesting. I do not think you were running MCC at the time.

Ms. HYDE. Yes.

The CHAIRMAN. And I know things have evolved, but can you say to us today that, again, this $800 million to a billion or whatever that is being spent——

Ms. HYDE. Yes.

The CHAIRMAN [continuing]. Outside of USAID is something that is creating transformative effects within these countries. And could you very briefly just name a couple of those transformative operations?

Ms. HYDE. Yes. Let me name five for you very briefly. The first I would mention is what is known as the MCC effect, that countries, particularly in Africa, where the penetration and the portfolio has been 65 percent over the decade, are striving to get to eligibility for MCC. And they are, in fact, changing their laws so that they can pass the scorecard so they can have compacts with MCC. We think that is very transformative. I know laws for women in Lesotho, and Cote d'Ivoire, and Sierra Leone, and other countries have been changed because of that.

Second, I mentioned the accountability framework. Over roughly a decade, MCC has signed 32 compacts with 26 countries. We have terminated assistance seven times. We have held countries accountable for maintaining their governance, not just at the front end, but through the duration of the compact. And I would say that that is a really notable, distinct accomplishment of a donor agency.

Third, in terms of economic rates of return, many agencies do not assess a cost benefit analysis. MCC does a very rigorous cost benefit analysis, and we do it before and after completion of a compact, in addition to independent evaluations.

So we're are looking at the front end for a 10 percent ERR. We have recently evaluated 58 projects—as of this month—that have closed. We are finding on average across that portfolio, the ERR at close out was 16 percent. So we are meeting those output targets.

Finally, I would just note in terms of building big infrastructure in the developing world, MCC in a decade has built a reputation on being able to design scope to the highest in some of the most difficult places on the globe, building roads, building bridges, building power transmissions facilities in a decade.

The CHAIRMAN. Well, I know when we go to countries like Pakistan and other places, they are constantly talking with us about these big signature projects that the Chinese and others are doing and we are not. So it is interesting you would point to that.

Let me ask just one last question, and I know we have two panels today. With respect to the threshold program and the issues of dealing with some of these projects, I understand you all are asking for 10 percent, and the President asked for less, and it has been around five percent. That, for what it is worth, feels very much like moving away from signature projects, moving away from transformative projects towards doing the same things, if you will, that USAID is doing.

So why would you venture into that territory when you just got through talking about doing things that are transformative?

Ms. HYDE. Yes, I appreciate the question. So MCC has essentially two product lines. On average, a compact over a decade has been roughly $350 million. The threshold size over a decade is roughly $22 million. The portfolio over the first decade was $10 billion, $9 and a half billion dollars put toward compacts in those 26 countries. Half a billion dollars against roughly as many threshold programs. The threshold program was significantly revised in 2012 and pared back. Right now, it is five percent of the portfolio. There are three countries that are actively implementing threshold programs, so it is very small.

I would say it is important, though, for these objectives: There are countries that start working with us, and I mentioned the MCC effect, this real sort of incentive effect for countries to get the gold standard, to get the Good Housekeeping Seal. There are countries that start years back—Cote d'Ivoire was one of them—and they are striving to make the scorecard and to make the changes, and they take many years.

Last year, Cote d'Ivoire's trend lines were up. They were on the cusp of being eligible for an MCC compact grant. And the board awarded them a threshold program to start, a very small investment so we could test their commitment, and so they could come forward with some sort of engagement, formal engagement with us. This year, a year later, the board will consider giving them a compact instead of that threshold program.

One of the important changes that we made in the threshold program is that a threshold program and a compact now both start with the constraints analysis, and that analysis takes about eight months, 10 months to complete between the economists of both countries. So there is no time lost in the fact that Cote d'Ivoire has been a threshold partner for a year. It will ripen, or may depending upon the decision of the board, into a compact partner. The same was true of Nepal, which started as a threshold partner and then became a compact partner.

So we think both from the ability to sort of test the waters with the partnership, and to do so in a small, limited way that does not lose any time or traction while we are engaged in the analytic exercise, that it makes sense in that context. And that is the context in which the threshold program is here today.

The CHAIRMAN. Thank you. Senator Cardin.

Senator CARDIN. Thank you very much for your leadership here. And I said in my opening statement, I am a strong supporter of MCC. I think it has been responsible for not only dealing with poverty issues, but also dealing with good governance issues and dealing with important security issues.

I know Jim Kolbe will be on the second panel. I was in the House and saw his work in his leadership position, recognizing how development assistance was critically important to U.S. security issues. And if there is a father of this program, it is Jim Kolbe, so it is nice to have Jim here, and I thank you very much for your continued interest in this area.

As you point out, there are performance indicators that need to be complied with, which is accountability, and it shows that we have real standards in order to decide where we will do a compact state. And you gave a good example on corruption—anticorruption efforts. But as I understand, I want to drill down a little bit more on this because I think we have learned over the course of the last decade that corruption is extremely difficult to deal with, and we need to leverage the best we can all of our programs.

My understanding is the indicator on anticorruption is basically a pass/fail grade based upon your relative efforts to your neighbors in the region, so you use a curve. We called that exam in college, you know, if you had a weak class you could get by. Is there a way that we can be more directive on any anticorruption activities?

It seems to me that we are developing universal standards that need to be met for a country to be serious in fighting corruption. No country will be corruption free, we know that, but there are good practices. And in certain regions, we need White House type of countries that are willing to really step forward.

Ms. HYDE. Yes.

Senator CARDIN. And it seems to me that the MCC could be helpful in that regard.

Ms. HYDE. Thank you, Senator, for the question. MCC is certainly seeking to drive a conversation among producers and consumers of corruption data about how we can continue to improve the data that we all use. What is interesting is that the business community very much is interested in sound data around corruption in countries and developing countries, and that there are a multitude of sources and producers for this. To that end, we have convened what is known as the Governance Data Alliance, which is seeking to improve this information, and we are doing a number of specific things under that umbrella.

I would say with respect to the median idea, it is the case that MCC is tracking corruption on an annual basis by the best indicator that we know, albeit imperfect. For indicators, our primary practical challenge is that we need an indicator that has global coverage, that can compare Nepal to Niger, and that is updated regularly on an annual basis. That in itself narrows the world for MCC as to what indicators actually meet those standards. And that is why these forums that we engage with to continually improve are very important.

The way it works, Senator, is that low-income countries, as defined by the World Bank, are judged against each other. That would be both Nepal and Niger. And lower-middle-income countries are judged against each other, and for both categories we are looking for countries above the median on each policy indicator. But importantly, we are looking at trend lines, and I think this is something that does get us a little bit beyond the pass/fail because we are looking at whether a country is on an upward trajectory over a period of years or a downward one, and both are significant as we think about decisionmaking.

Senator CARDIN. Well, I thank you for that answer. I would just point out by comparison, we are looking—this committee is looking at global standards on fighting corruption. We have learned our lessons from trafficking. We have objective standards of how countries need to deal with trafficking issues. Each country is different, but we have universal standards that the United States has developed. And, no, it is not a passing or failing. We do have gradations there.

And I understand you have to make a decision, but I do hope that you would be more aggressive because to me, this is one of the most difficult areas, that fight for good governance. So improving in this area I think would be important.

I want to move on to the regional compact and the legislation that we have brought forward. There is a great deal of interest in this. You mentioned Nepal and India are looking at ways that they can either deal with transportation or energy on a regional basis and which the compact could be very helpful. And in East Africa and West Africa, Senator Coons has been talking a good deal about projects in those regions where we have compact countries individual, but if we could do it collectively, we might be able to get further along on that. And in our own hemisphere in Central America we have a compact country, but we could do more. Similar problems on trade. Similar problems on transportation, energy, et cetera.

So if you had that authority, how would you use the evaluation process—considering that the performance indicators are country specific, how do you deal with that if you had regional authority? How do we know that we still will be able to get the same type of progress, leveraging, of private sector investment, and accountability if you had regional authority?

Ms. HYDE. Thank you, Senator, I appreciate the question. As you mentioned, the theory of the case in today's global economy for regional investments is quite strong, particularly when you have a tool of U.S. development whose only mission is economic growth, fighting poverty through growth. So we believe that theory has been proven.

The challenge is more in the logistics and the operational complexity of this. MCC would maintain the same standards; that is, for the scorecard and for approval. So we would be looking at those few places on the globe where there are contiguous countries, next to each other, who are passing the scorecard, who are fairly stable in passing the scorecard, and who themselves are looking for opportunities to integrate.

I think our starting point for this could likely be in Africa. I say that because MCC is a brand and an asset of the United States that is well known in Africa, particularly in West Africa where the penetration of our portfolio has been the greatest. And we see, be it through Senegal, Cote d'Ivoire, Ghana, a number of investments that we have made that perhaps could have had a higher value if we would have thought about how to cross borders. It may be in energy. It may be in transportation.

The implementation modality, I think we would continue—we have to continue to make this a country-led enterprise. And we have done that through accountable entities that are created. In this case, it would need to be across borders that would work together. And we would have to be mindful of the idea that if there was a governance stumble in one of the countries, we would have to bifurcate and sever that investment and still make part of that investment valuable. But our eyes are wide open about those challenges.

Ten years ago, I would not have recommended that MCC launch into this space. Today, I think it is uniquely positioned for the reasons that you have mentioned. First of all, the credibility capital. Not that we have it everywhere, but we have it in some regions where we have had large penetration.

Second of all, the fact is that MCC has worked in infrastructure, in power and roads, and that is vital. This is what we are lookinf for in these countries. And third, because MCC's instrument is grant assistance, and you mentioned the private sector, these deals will not get done without private investment, and there is some debt financing out there as well. The grant assistance could be what actually pulls the private sector investment deals together with the United States involvement. So I think those are three reasons why it could work.

Senator CARDIN. Thank you.

The CHAIRMAN. Senator Flake.

Senator FLAKE. Thank you, and thank you for the testimony, and thank you for what you are doing at MCC.

With regard to these regional compacts, I am happy to be part of the legislation giving the authority, and I hope we can get it through. Can you talk about Southern Africa? There are some possibilities with Zambia——

Ms. HYDE. Yes.

Senator FLAKE [continuing]. Tanzania, Malawi. What are we looking at there?

Ms. HYDE. In that area of the region in particular, we think there are interesting power opportunities, certainly between Zambia and Tanzania. There is also the need for water infrastructure, and agriculture and irrigation, as well as road and border crossings. So those three countries, as well, are countries that we have worked with such as Mozambique, have scoped out in a very broad sense what are some potential projects to work there. We are in the very early stages of this. We would need copious diligence on each one of them before selecting where we would go.

Senator FLAKE. Can you tell us about kind of the intersection between MCC and our Power Africa initiative that is being undertaken now?

Ms. HYDE.Yes. So MCC, as I mentioned before, undertakes at the front end, a constraints-to-growth analysis, and that is conducted by economists usually from the finance ministry of whatever country with which we are partnering together with MCC's economists. It takes upwards of a year, and at the end of that, there is a high-level buy in of what the binding constraints are to growth.

What we have seen for quite some time is that energy poverty, the lack of reliable electricity, is again and again a binding constraint to growth in Africa. So that is the premise through which the MCC is part of Power Africa. It is under that principle that our engagement is to be a country-led program. And I have had more than one head of state of an African country call me directly and ask me specifically to engage in energy.

I would say the third element to what these countries and these partnerships are asking for is they want American private sector investment, and they see a lot of opportunities in energy through that as well. So we are a participant in Power Africa, but we are doing so under the MCC model.

Senator FLAKE. Following on one of the questions that Senator Cardin had about some of the challenges with these regional compacts, suppose you have two countries enter into a compact for some electricity project or power generation project. One country has a coup two years later into the compact. What do we do?

Ms. HYDE. We scope and design an investment at the front end that takes account of that possibility, looks at economic rates of return if we were to undertake the interventions on just one side of the border or the other. The assumption is that there will be greater returns if we do it across the border, but I still would think we could not do a project that was nothing in terms of its own value to the country because of that possibility.

So I think it is a challenge in design and in due diligence, and certainly a risk assessment of where we select countries for regional investments. If MCC were to receive this authority, I think we would be cautious, start slowly, not undertake a lot at the front end, and prove the concept.

Senator FLAKE. So there is a political risk analysis done——

Ms. HYDE. Yes. Yes.

Senator FLAKE [continuing]. Working with the State Department and other agencies.

Ms. HYDE. Absolutely. Absolutely.

Senator FLAKE. All right. Thank you. Thank you, Mr. Chairman.

The CHAIRMAN. Thank you. Senator Menendez.

Senator MENENDEZ. Thank you, Mr. Chairman. Ms. Hyde, let me—I want to pursue a line of questioning so I understand some of the apportionment of MCC. I have been a strong supporter of it since its creation. But I look at development assistance as a whole, and whatever we do at MCC we know AID and other elements are affected by it, and I think MCC has done great work.

But my understanding is that the MCC board has approved 33 compacts in 26 countries totaling about $11 billion. Is that about right?

Ms. HYDE. My number I have is 32, but I would be happy to figure out what the discrepancy is there, yes.

Senator MENENDEZ. Okay. How about the other parts, about 26 countries?

Ms. HYDE. 26 countries, 32 compacts. Over the decade, roughly $10 billion in year 11, about $11 billion. So year to date, yes.

Senator MENENDEZ. Now, of that, MCC's 32, 33 signed compacts, 19 are with African countries spanning the continent. Is that a fair statement?

Ms. HYDE. Yes.

Senator MENENDEZ. So that from my calculations totals about $7.4 billion or about 67 percent of MCC's total compact portfolio.

Ms. HYDE. Yes.

Senator MENENDEZ. So I have been a strong supporter of development in Africa. I think it is an incredibly important continent in many different iterations to U.S. interests. But I would like to understand then the breakdown for other regions.

If roughly two-thirds of the MCC's efforts are directed to Africa, that leaves one-third for the remainder of the world—Latin America, which I have a great interest in, the Middle East, the former Soviet Union, Asia. So can you talk to me about the factors that you all assess? I mean, I am familiar with the MCC. with what you need to qualify, but how do you all go about looking at the world in the context of your focus? What factors describe the disproportionality, and are you all looking at this as part of your overall evaluation about where you are working in the world?

Ms. HYDE. Thank you, Senator. I appreciate the question. I would be happy to tell you how we got to that. The starting point for selection and eligibility under the statute is that MCC is to

work with low-income and lower-middle-income countries as defined by the World Bank. That is roughly a GNI of zero to 2,000
dollars per capita, and 2,000 to 4,000 dollars per capita.

Ten years ago, there were 113 countries in the globe that fit this
definition. Today there are 81, so there has been about a 30 percent reduction. Those 81 countries are mainly in Africa, but some
are elsewhere in the globe. But I know, for example, South America
has some very poor countries, so that is a starting point. From
there, MCC is to apply the scorecard, which is a filter that has a
hard hurdle around corruption and a hard hurdle around democracy. Those are two must pass indicators. And then the other indicators, countries must pass 10 indicators overall on the 20 indicator scorecard.

This year, in FY 2016, there are 29 countries that passed the
scorecard. Roughly eight of them are small islands with less than
a million people. So the MCC selection process through the filters
that are both in statute and through the scorecard, which is critical
to our accountability framework, filtering out much of the globe.
That said, MCC has worked in all three of the Northern Triangle
countries: in Guatemala, Honduras, and in El Salvador. In fact, is
two are currently in our smaller threshold program and we have
a compact with El Salvador.

The Board selections for new compacts last December were all
outside of Africa. The Board selected Nepal, Mongolia, and the
Philippines as partners, and we see countries rising in Southeast
Asia. But the result of where we are working is in large measure
the combination of the candidate pool as defined by statute as well
as the scorecard.

Senator MENENDEZ. So if 81 countries in the world are potentially qualified in the first instance, and that whittles down to 29
after the filtering of your standards, and eight of them are small
islands of less than a million people, that is about 21 countries that
actually can be considered.

Ms. HYDE. Yes.

Senator MENENDEZ. And so, I would like to get from you, and not
necessarily at this moment——

Ms. HYDE. Sure.

Senator MENENDEZ [continuing]. But I would like to get from you
what are those 21 countries because you have to look at a billion
dollars and think about what is it that you are doing vis-à-vis the
universe of who is eligible, because if at the end of the day only
a certain universe is eligible, then I look at development assistance
as it relates to the amount of money versus the universe that I can
potentially spend it in.

Even though I believe MCC standards are incredibly important——

Ms. HYDE. Yes.

Senator MENENDEZ [continuing]. I also know that the development pot is limited at the end of the day.

Ms. HYDE. Yes.

Senator MENENDEZ. And that may affect how I or others might
look at what USAID does separate and apart from MCC and how
their focus should be, so that when we put it all together, we understand the development in the world because I see within the

Western Hemisphere maybe a limited number of countries that meet both the standards and the filtering. But I see some great needs, as is evidenced by the fact of, you know, citizens' security, children coming to the United States. I see a real impact on U.S. interests as a result of that, and I do not see us——

And I look at AID and the cuts on AID to Latin America. So I say, okay, so what are we doing about the hemisphere in which we live in and in which we have a direct interest in terms of our security, our economics because citizens of the Western Hemisphere most likely will seek American products and services more so than in other parts of the globe. And we have a population problem as it relates to those who seek refuge, either from violence of their governments or violence of gangs and other—and narco trafficking and whatnot.

I am a strong supporter of the MCC. I do not want you to get me wrong. But I am trying to look at the total development dollars in figuring out how we look at that as it relates to our needs. And so, in that context, I look forward to your answer.

Ms. HYDE. I would be happy to follow up.

[The information referred to can be found on page 93, at the end of this transcript.]

Senator MENENDEZ. Thank you.

Ms. HYDE. I would be happy to follow up with you specifically. I should have clarified that with respect to those 21 countries, MCC has already engaged with many of them, so many of them are already current partners. Relatively few new partners would be one point to that, but I am happy to provide you with a list specifically of what they are for you to take a look at.

In addition to that, I would just say, raising a more global point, that we know over the decade that there has been a shift in the landscape of poverty. MCC's only mission is to address poverty through growth. And poverty looks different than it did 10 years ago, so there may be reasons to re-look at what that landscape is and how we measure it. And we would welcome the opportunity to engage on that.

The CHAIRMAN. And when you say that, when you say it is different, you mean there less poverty today than 10 years ago. Is that what you are saying?

Ms. HYDE. There absolutely—there is less of it. There are also more concentrations, as you have heard, in urban areas and in cities. There is also—the particular measure that we use by statute looks at GNI as opposed to individuals, households, and pockets of poverty. And so, mineral wealth and natural resource wealth can raise a country's GNI when there is a very large percentage of that population living under two dollars a day.

So I think you may hear more about this in the second panel, but I think it is worth examining.

The CHAIRMAN. Senator Perdue.

Senator PERDUE. Well, Ms. Hyde, thank you. I really fully respect what you are doing. God bless you for doing it.

Ms. HYDE. Thank you.

Senator PERDUE. I have just four quick questions, and I would love if the first two would be hopefully quick answers. But, you know, let me try to put this in perspective.

In 1965, we had—we started basically the War on Poverty in the United States, and unfortunately today the poverty rate is basically the same as it was when we signed the Great Society. In addition to that, in the last seven years, just to pick seven years when our debt has really sort of skyrocketed, we have spent about $125 billion between USAID and MCC. These are round numbers and directionally correct.

And of that $125 billion, we borrowed $50 billion. So that means that 40 percent of every billion dollars we spend with MCC every year, we have to go to China, and Japan, to our own Federal Reserve to fund that. And so, every dime that we spend is very critical.

In addition to that, though, I will say we have got a model, and that is Lee Kwan Yew in Singapore, based on four things—water, power, infrastructure, and educated workforce—went from a swamp to a major economy today. So I think you are on the right track. I love your mission, reducing poverty through economic growth. I heard, though, just a minute ago American values slipped in there, and I want to come back to later. I know that is one of the prerequisites, but I am concerned about that.

Let me just ask a couple of questions. I am chair of this subcommittee, and you and I are going to get to know each a lot over the next couple of years I hope.

Ms. HYDE. Okay.

Senator PERDUE. And I fully respect what you do. But to whom do you report?

Ms. HYDE. I report to a board that is both the public and private sector, nine members, five——

Senator PERDUE. But who oversees that board?

Ms. HYDE. Secretary Kerry.

Senator PERDUE. Thank you. And of the 68 programs you are talking about, the compacts, about $3 billion, 16 percent internal rate of return. I would love that if I were you, that is good, over that. But what has been the poverty reduction of those 58 compacts?

Ms. HYDE. Well, the evaluations of many are still under way. Cost benefit, we are looking at dollars we actually spent at close out, and our projections of beneficiaries. We are independently evaluating 100 percent of the program, and those valuations, I do not know if the alignment is between the 58. We have about 50 that have been completed.

In terms of results of those independent impact evaluations, MCC has set the bar higher than outputs, which is—often sometimes inputs are measured. There are outputs. We are looking to see if we can find income raises for——

Senator PERDUE. So in 10 years, we do not have any programs where we can measure the impact on poverty?

Ms. HYDE. We have 50 programs that have undertaken rigorous outside independent evaluations, and these are projects.

Senator PERDUE. Right.

Ms. HYDE. We have a mixed record, and for many reasons we think, so far. We have seen income raises in some of our agricultural projects in Ghana, farming projects. We have seen with respect to the roads, for example—let me just give you an example quickly. We——

Senator PERDUE. I am sorry to interrupt. I know these are anecdotal examples, and they are great. I fully respect that. One of the concerns I have is you spent a billion dollars across X number of compacts. Did we really spend enough in any one country to really have an impact on poverty? And if so, why can we not measure it? You may not be able to answer today, but that is where I am going in the future is to say, okay——

Ms. HYDE. In fact, whether it is enough——

Senator PERDUE [continuing]. If that is our mission, let us get there. You guys do a great job of quantitative evaluation. I will give you high marks on that. I am concerned about a couple of anecdotal incidents, though. I visited your team in Indonesia and Jakarta. Very impressive people, great hearts. But I was very troubled that over half the money we are spending in Indonesia is spent on a green power project. I do not remember the name of it, and it had no cost benefit analysis. And then in Tanzania, another about $285 billion, or million rather, spent on a similar project that had no cost benefit analysis on the front end.

Can you help me with why those energy projects in two different instances did not have a cost benefit analysis?

Ms. HYDE. Thank you, and I will try to be quick because I know you are trying to get through a lot.

Senator PERDUE. Well, it is your time now. You can go on.

Ms. HYDE. Well, I did not know if there were more ERRs in Indonesia. In Indonesia, we did it more as a financing facility that wants to have private sector match, so we could not do a cost benefit because we did not know what the calls for proposals would bring in. So the way that is working is that it is mostly small and medium enterprises. It is in rural Indonesia.

We have signed a dozen plus of them. Each one of them has had a matching component from the private sector.

Senator PERDUE. But basically these were green energy production.

Ms. HYDE. In our selection of projects we are doing ERRs. We are doing them. We just did not do them at the front end because we actually did not know what projects we were going to fund. It was the financing facility.

In Tanzania, we have not—the board has not approved that compact. That compact will not be approved without the ERRs. There is data under way. Clearly not going to happen in the——

Senator PERDUE. So the question is, when we look at an enterprise like that in Indonesia in a business, you would look at alternatives, right, and see which one had the best.

Ms. HYDE. Yes. Yes. Yes.

Senator PERDUE. So you are looking at a green project, and therein lies one of my concerns about American value in the intervention in that in your very high regarded mission of reducing poverty through economic growth.

Ms. HYDE. Sure.

Senator PERDUE. I can do one, but when the other gets in the way of this, then I have to say that is a constraint that helps me or hinders me in reaching my objective.

Ms. HYDE. Yes, I——

Senator PERDUE. So in Indonesia, I am concerned about that one point because I have been in those villages. I have operated factories in Indonesia. They need power, there is no question. Putting a green power generating unit in there may not be the most cost effective. So did you look at alternative ways to get power in that community or those communities?

Ms. HYDE. In Indonesia, we started with the constraints analysis. We worked with a core team of Indonesians who themselves were putting on the table that they wanted to look at renewable sources of energy. I think the constraints spoke quite a bit about the degradation of the land outside of the capital around these issues, and that it was the Indonesians' idea to come forward and do this.

From an American values perspective, to the extent I use that phrase, it is often in connection with the scorecard. So top line values of good governance, corruption, rule of law, very much reflective. I did not mean to speak to that in terms of the context of a program because the programs are, and this is much more challenging quite candidly, very much a country within an accountability framework.

Senator PERDUE. Right. Thank you.

Ms. HYDE. So that is——

Senator PERDUE. Yes. One last question. We spend about a billion dollars in MCC and about $17 billion in USAID.

Ms. HYDE. Yes.

Senator PERDUE. And I think both have about the same overhead. It is about 10 percent. But you have a little more review and monitoring, I think, expense than maybe USAID. You are teaching people to fish instead of just giving them fish, so there is a fundamental difference. I get that.

Help me with the fact that given the earlier conversation that we had, why MCC? What is different here? I understand you have two different, you said products, I think, or efforts. Why could not that be or why can that not be housed inside a bureaucracy that we already have?

Ms. HYDE. Well, I think both are critical. I think they are very different models, both being MCC and USAID. Top line, USAID is across the globe. MCC is working with roughly two dozen high performing countries, using objective standards. Second of all, MCC is only focused on growth, and that is a multi-sectoral approach in a country mix that is going to look different in every country because of the third principle of country-led and how important it is to teach them to fish.

As you know, we do not work in humanitarian assistance, conflict, refugee relief. We do not set global targets for health, global targets for education. We are looking at those countries and looking to burrow deep and go deep into the platform.

So those are top line differences between USAID and MCC. We are extremely lean. I mentioned that there are 300 professionals at MCC undertaking this whole program. When we have that program on the ground, there will be two people from America for MCC, and there will be Indonesians leading that program, with a board of Indonesians managing the program. So it is a very distinct model.

Senator PERDUE. Good. Good answer. I really, again, applaud what you are doing. Thank you.

Ms. HYDE. Thank you.

Senator PERDUE. I look forward to working with you.

Ms. HYDE. Thank you.

Senator PERDUE. Thank you.

The CHAIRMAN. Before we turn to Senator Coons——

Ms. HYDE. Yes.

The CHAIRMAN.—I just think since we have another panel that is coming up, with some who support MCC some who do not. I think we left something hanging there, and I appreciate the line of questioning. But you mentioned American values relative to the scorecard. Yes/no answer. Are there are any pressures on MCC to be involved in projects that really in some cases have something more to do with pursuing a social purpose than with just basic economic growth for the citizens there? Yes/no.

Ms. HYDE. No, there is a database of everything—evidence base for everything MCC is doing. I mean, that is—MCC is—I am not, Senator—Mr. Chairman, what you mean by social purpose.

The CHAIRMAN. I think you understood what the questioning was. It sounded like that maybe energy projects were being pursued that were maybe not economical, if you will, and not pursued as driving towards economic growth as otherwise might have been the case. You just need to answer that "yes" or "no" because it will become an issue.

Ms. HYDE. No. I was told particularly in Indonesia, diesel is very expensive. So we are looking at cost benefit. We are looking at what the country wants. I would say the two principles are whether the constraints analysis has led us there, and whether the country, the Indonesia team, is putting these ideas on the table. So this is—that is how we get to what we are doing.

The CHAIRMAN. Senator Coons.

Senator COONS. Thank you, Chairman Corker, Ranking Member Cardin, for convening this hearing. And, Ms. Hyde, great to see you again. I have had the opportunity to visit MCC projects on the ground in Ghana, in Benin, in Senegal, in Cabo Verde, in Tanzania. And I have to say your model, what MCC has been doing since launched by leaders in Congress and the Bush administration. I am a huge supporter. I am convinced that it is a different way to do development.

Senator Perdue just cited some very large numbers in terms of our foreign aid spend, the vast majority of which is on Iraq, Afghanistan, Israel, Pakistan. You are a very small part of our total foreign aid spend, and with a very different model as I have seen it, and as you laid out, very data driven. Very analytically based with a very light footprint. Country ownership, country leadership, longer-term partnerships. I think one that in the places that I have visited allows us to compete directly with China by being a partner in designing, delivering, and developing quality infrastructure.

Not quantity infrastructure. Not massive projects. For example the port in Benin that I visited, the power generation project, out to Zanzibar. What I saw in up country Ghana with Senator Isakson were quality infrastructure projects.

But most importantly, in my view, is what you call the MCC effect. I cannot tell you how many African heads of state have lobbied me personally on trying to get into MCC without having to meet the indicators around corruption, or transparency, or media. And I am just going to take off for a moment on that point about American values.

In a data driven analytical, transparent way that tries to crowd in private investment, you are, in my view, advancing some of our most core American values, which are that economic growth is sustainable when it occurs in an environment of transparency, rule of law, respect for right, and where corruption is persistently tackled. So I do think you are advancing American values, but not in a way that is outside of these indicators.

The thing I mostly want to discuss—and I do agree with Senator Menendez's point. I advocate for MCC in Appropriations. I wish there were a broader, more robust funding stream to allow a broader range of compacts. The good news is that over the last decade, extreme poverty has been reduced, and the number of countries you can work with has gone down. So your focus is overwhelmingly on Africa in recent years where deep poverty remains.

I am conscious of situations in Southern Africa, East Africa, West Africa where there is very little trade between countries, and these are not large countries. Many of them trade more with Europe than they do with each other, with countries literally 50 miles or 100 miles away.

Just walk through one more time—I am grateful for Senator Cardin's leadership on this EMCOR bill. Why will regional compact authority allow you to accelerate what your model has made possible, and what are your intentions in terms of dealing with some legitimate questions raised by Senator Flake, Senator Corker, and others about the risks inherent in going into a slight expansion—an expansion of the model that would allow you to engage with several countries at once in a commonly designed project?

Ms. HYDE. Thank you, Senator Coons. So let me try and tackle that quickly. You know, as I mentioned, the economies of scale argument that you referenced, Africa—let us take Africa, 54 fragmented, very small markets. At the time, the largest and fastest-rising middle class on the globe. In terms of the opportunity for American businesses, six of the 10 fastest-growing economies.

Africa itself is seeking and has really made some progress over the last couple of decades in terms of the political will to undertake integration. This is something that we heard from the African Union, certainly in Gabon, and I spoke to many finance ministers about this directly.

What they need now is the support on the infrastructure. There is both the hard side and the soft side to getting to regional integration in Africa. There is obviously harmonization of tariff structures and reforms, as well as building those roads and building those border crossings and whatnot.

I think MCC is viewed in Africa as a—I am speaking generally here, but as a trusted partner of the United States that can help bridge both sides of that, both the soft considerations as well as the hard considerations. I certainly know from speaking with the private sector that the project prep funds, as well as viability gap financing, is what could help make these deals possible.

I do not expect that MCC's portfolio would balloon in regional work because it is so hard. So as I said earlier, I think MCC has to be very careful about the countries we pick, about the sector and the project that we pick, and start slowly and responsibly to prove the concept because there is obviously that component of it here.

Senator COONS. Well, in my experience in Africa, it is striking that the lines on the map that divide countries were often drawn fairly arbitrarily a century ago by European powers. And so, they do not rationally reflect where water systems are, where transpor- tation systems are, where population centers are, or where econo- mies are growing, and they remain real constraints. And our en- gaged, thoughtful leadership that is outcomes oriented and data driven can pull together regional markets in terms of energy and infrastructure.

The private sector investors I talked to, and I just met the other day with one of the biggest French banks that invests heavily in Africa, they are looking for markets of scale, and they are looking for improvements in transparency and in rule of law. We can help deliver that, and I think this is a great bill, and I look forward to supporting it, and appreciate your testimony and your hard work.

Ms. HYDE. Thank you, Senator.

The CHAIRMAN. Thank you. Thank you very much. Senator Kaine.

Senator KAINE. Thank you, Mr. Chairman. Thank you, Ms. Hyde. I want to return to a line of questioning from Senator Menendez about the Northern Triangle, and I want to kind of use the Northern Triangle as an example.

I actually think the Northern Triangle is a great example of why regional compacts would make a lot of sense. We know that we are dealing with a lot of policy issues in the Northern Triangle—unaccompanied minors, violence—some of it driven by frankly U.S. citizens' demand for drugs. So it is not just that the problems there affect us, but our own problems affect those communities, so there is a connection that is a significant one.

I am kind of puzzled by why in the Northern Triangle there is one compact and then two thresholds. And so, just in terms of the metrics, I mean, all of these countries have challenges. One of the original motives of MCC was to focus on free market economics, and the country that has the compact is probably the one where the private sector most feels suppressed by the government, El Sal- vador. I am not saying El Salvador should not have a compact. I am supportive, but I think it is interesting as you look at Guate- mala and Honduras, their private sectors probably feel a little more included by the government than the private sector in El Salvador. So I think if you do not move to a regional, you are going to end up with weird anomalies like that. Can you explain that anomaly in the Northern Triangle?

Ms. HYDE. Yes. So I think the Northern Triangle outside of Afri- ca is, I agree with you, completely—one of the best examples of the potential and the opportunity for regional investments. Indeed, we have looked at some of the road segments that we have built in those countries or supported in other ways, and pondered over the opportunity if we just were connecting those roads in and of themselves. So it provides a very vivid map.

To answer your question specifically on the threshold program, Guatemala has seen improvements in its scorecard, and as of last year I believe was the median country, which is just below passing in terms of the control of corruption indicator. Obviously there were the events of the past year with the election and the new administration. I was there early in the year at the signing of the threshold program. They have not yet passed the scorecard, but if there is a positive trajectory, then they could be a candidate for an upcoming board meeting. On Honduras, we had a strong partnership with Honduras.

Senator KAINE. Because they were a compact country originally.

Ms. HYDE. They were a compact country. They experienced political violence as well as at the same time transitioned from a low-income to a lower-middle-income country, so they were being evaluated against a different peer set. And their scorecard went down precipitously.

Senator KAINE. I see.

Ms. HYDE. So those were the two factors that led us to move and transition Honduras to Threshold.

Senator KAINE. But the point that you made about the regional compact, the funding has supported transportation infrastructure in all three countries, and it would be so much better because these are nations that do trade with one another——

Ms. HYDE. Yes. Yes.

Senator KAINE [continuing]. If the transportation could link up instead of being kind of just country specific.

Ms. HYDE. I would share one more fact on that, which is, as you know, the leaders of those nations last year came forward with their own program, the Alliance for Progress, to address the root causes of instability that were leading to the unaccompanied minors issue. And what is interesting about the statement that they put out is because each one of them have worked with MCC, they know the MCC model that has a board and local staff and has them undertaking the implementation under these controls, and that the last line of that statement, the leaders themselves said if we are to undertake this program jointly, they would implement it with the MCC model, not referring to MCC assistance, but essentially referring to the doing it the MCC way.

To me, that was one of the best reflections of a country-led approach that they would take on and adopt for their own if that is how they perceive it.

Senator KAINE. Right, and that is an additional point about the regional compact there. They are trying to act regionally in putting a plan on the table.

Second question is sort of about the coordination of MCC with other forms of aid. So the President in his introduced budget asked for a billion dollars for Plan Central America to basically help those three nations with security, governance, economic development challenges. The appropriations process will produce whatever number it produces.

But I am kind of interested, how will we try to leverage whatever is the dollar amount that is appropriated for Plan Central America and the three countries with the MCC involvement in the three countries, because to kind of have just, you know, competing or separate programs might not, again, leverage the dollars to achieve the maximum effect.

So from the MCC standpoint, you know, Plan Central America gets funded at X level. What would you do to try to make sure that the work being done in the three nations gets the biggest bang for the bucks?

Ms. HYDE. I appreciate the question. So, first, I would say that we have done a constraints-to-growth analysis in each one of those countries, and that we have shared that analysis. In fact, El Salvador is part of the broader administration effort on partnership for growth. MCC was—and we will share the constraints anywhere, but—actively working with others to say here is what we have identified in the United States government. Here is what we have identified as binding constraints-to-growth. Here is what we are able to tackle. Here are other pieces for that.

And I think that approach is a value, a public good that MCC brings to the table both in this region and with the U.S. Government, but also with the other donor community, the way that we can put within that framework those results. So we would work closely if those programs do materialize. I would say right now with the El Salvador compact, we are one of the most concentrated and largest donors seeking to address those root causes of instability there, and would work closely with other partners.

Senator KAINE. Great. Thank you. Thank you, Mr. Chairman.

Ms. HYDE. Thank you.

The CHAIRMAN. We thank you very much for your testimony and your leadership, and I am sure there will be some follow-up questions that people will ask. Hopefully you will answer those promptly.

And with that, if you would like to go about your business, that would be good. [Laughter.]

And we will bring up another panel, okay? Thank you so much. Thank you.

Ms. HYDE. Thank you. Thank you, Mr. Chairman. Thank you.

The CHAIRMAN. If the other panel would come on up.

I would now like to recognize the witnesses that we have for the second panel. The first witness is the Honorable James Kolbe, senior transatlantic fellow at the German Marshall Fund of the U.S. And, Jim, while we have not worked together, I know you had a distinguished career here in Congress. My staff alluded the same credit to you relative to the creation of MCC, and I want to thank you for all your involvement and for being here today as a witness. It is much appreciated. I am sure Senator Cardin will want to say even more since he served with you.

The second witness is the Honorable Andrew Natsios, director of the Scowcroft Institute of International Affairs and executive professor at the Bush School of Government and Public Service at Texas A&M. I want to thank you for being here. We appreciate that.

And our third witness will be Dr. Nancy Birdsall, president of the Center for Global Development. Thank you so much.

I think you all understand, it would help if you could summarize your remarks in five minutes. Without objection, your written testimony will be entered into the record, and Senator Cardin and I and others look forward to questioning.

Why don't we just start and go through the order in which I introduced you, if that is okay. And I do not know if you want to say anything by way of introduction.

Senator CARDIN. I will reserve. I just really want to point out with Jim Kolbe, during the time of his leadership in the House, it was a period where development assistance was extremely difficult to support. I think there is greater understanding today about the importance of development assistance. But Jim Kolbe was the leader in the House of Representatives for connecting the importance of U.S. engagement internationally on the development assistance program. So, Jim, it is wonderful to have you back here.

The CHAIRMAN. So if you would start. Thank you again for being here, sir.

STATEMENT OF HON. JAMES KOLBE, SENIOR TRANSATLANTIC FELLOW, THE GERMAN MARSHALL FUND OF THE UNITED STATES, WASHINGTON, DC

Mr. KOLBE. Thank you, Mr. Chairman, and Ranking Member Cardin, thank you especially for your very generous remarks, overly generous remarks, I should say, about my role in all of this. But I am pleased to be here. I think it is a wonderful opportunity to testify on the subject of the Millennium Challenge Corporation. It is an important, it is a timely hearing as the MCC passes its 10-year mark. And I want to commend the CEO, Ms. Dana Hyde, for looking ahead and for her commitment to keeping the Agency at the forefront of what I consider to be good development practice. I am also delighted to be joined by my distinguished colleagues on this panel, Andrew Natsios and Dr. Nancy Birdsall, with whom I have worked on various occasions. And I will not go more into detail because of the limited time here.

As Senator Cardin pointed out, in 2004, the Foreign Operations Subcommittee of Policy Appropriations, which I chaired at that time, worked to pass with strong bipartisan support the legislation creating the Millennium Challenge Corporation. MCC did represent a new approach to foreign assistance with a radical departure from the way programs had been designed and countries designated for foreign assistance in the past. It was designed with the singular mission of reducing poverty through economic growth in the world's poorest, but relatively well-governed countries.

The MCC's model of assistance is focused on four solemn principles: first, selectivity in determining which countries that ought to partner based on agreed upon criteria, objectively measured and objectively applied; second, a business-like approach to choosing investments; third a focus on country ownership; fourth, a rigorous commitment to transparency and accountability.

MCC partners must demonstrate a commitment to ruling justly, investing in their people, and supporting democratic rights. Over its decade-long existence, the MCC has demonstrated, I believe, that this model does work. By working exclusively with countries that demonstrate commitment to good governance, the rule of law, and of economic freedom, the MCC has had the multiplying effective of compelling low-income countries, even those who do not currently partner with the Millennium Challenge Corporation, to reform institutions, change laws, improve how they operate in order to try to qualify for MCC assistance, what was called the MCC effect that you heard about earlier.

As we peer over the horizon of the next 10 years, I want to offer just a couple of reflections on how I think MCC can continue to stay on the cutting edge of development while remaining true to its original intent. First, there is always going to be a temptation by policymakers in the executive branch and here in Congress to allow new priorities to interfere with MCC's core values.

The MCC should not allow itself to succumb to other considerations, strategic or otherwise, that are inconsistent with or run counter to MCC's fundamental approach. Long-term development requires focus and discipline. It cannot and should not be an instrument of day-to-day diplomatic engagement or set aside in order to respond to the political crisis of the day.

What has made the MCC successful has been its unwavering commitment to the principles upon which it was founded—democracy, rule of law, good governance, and transparency—principles that are deeply embedded in the American value system. But a desire for democratic decisionmaking to have a government free of corruption, to be shielded by the adherence to the rule of law, these are not exclusively American values. Other countries want them as well.

When the MCC was established, it included in the founding legislation a private sector component of the MCC's board, four private sector members. These members have worked in a bipartisan fashion in years that have passed in successive administrations to honor the MCC's mandate by maintaining the rightful focus on the MCC's development objectives, even when confronted with sometimes unrelated policy priorities and emergencies.

Second, I think the MCC model has always been built on the idea of partnerships with developing countries, setting the course of engagement. The MCC has integrated a number of requested steps to foster inclusiveness and accountability. I am confident with the passage of time we will find that one of the long-term benefits of the MCC will prove to be its ability to strengthen the citizen state compact.

Third, the MCC has been a pioneer on transparency, publishing the data elements from the start of compact through to its completion. This dogged adherence to openness ensures accountability both for U.S. taxpayers and for the citizens of participating countries.

I applaud the MCC's interest in concurrent compact authority. I will not go into detail. You had a good discussion of that with the CEO here. But I think that the concurrent compacts would allow the MCC to break up in implementation the compact components between Fiscal Years. Such authority would provide more flexibility to the existing 5-year model employed by MCC. The MCC explicitly has legal authority to negotiate co-investment agreements with the private sector. Public-private partnerships are necessary for the MCC to achieve its mission in an era of limited government resources.

MCC's control corruption indicator needs to be strengthened, allowing for greater distinction between those countries that are meeting the criteria and those that are not. Good governance does not equate to lack of corruption. Better data is needed for the MCC corruption index.

The MCC also needs to take a closer look at low-income countries and the lower-middle-income-countries categories to ensure that we are targeting the right set of countries with our assistance. As you just heard, the world has changed since MCC was created. Thankfully the pool of countries that are at the economic bottom is shrinking, and so we need to look today to see whether the 25 percent cap on funds for the lower-middle-income countries is appropriate in today's world.

So these are just a few of the things that I would mention to you. In conclusion, let me just say that I believe that the MCC has shown itself to be a game changer in how we look at development assistance, engage partner countries, and achieve meaningful development outcomes that are measurable and clear. After 10 years, it is only appropriate that you look at today how the Agency is working and how it can be strengthened to do even better. But I am convinced that given the attributes of the MCC and its performance-driven mission, I have no doubt that it will remain up to the challenge. And I look forward to answering any questions you might have.

[The prepared statement of Mr. Kolbe follows:]

PREPARED STATEMENT OF JIM KOLBE

Chairman Corker, Ranking Member Cardin, and members of the Committee: Thank you for the opportunity to testify today on the subject of the Millennium Challenge Corporation. This is an important and timely agency for your consideration, as the MCC recently passed its 10-year mark and is currently developing a new 5-year strategic plan. I would like to commend MCC CEO Dana Hyde for her looking ahead and her commitment to keep the agency at the forefront of good development practice.

I am also delighted to be joined by my distinguished colleagues on this panel. I worked with Andrew Natsios when he ably served as administrator of the United States Agency for International Development under President Bush while I was chairman of the House Appropriations Subcommittee on Foreign Operations and Related Agencies, and more recently together as members of the Consensus for Development Reform, which aims to strengthen U.S. global leadership through reforming and improving our approach to global development. I've also had the pleasure of working with Nancy Birdsall in numerous capacities, including jointly serving on the Transatlantic Taskforce on Development at the German Marshall Fund, which produced a report examining key issues around the role of development assistance. Nancy remains a respected thought leader on development. While she recently announced she plans to step down from her leadership post at the Center for Global Development next year, I know she will continue to be an intellectual force and leading voice on the future of development.

MCC: IN TEN SHORT YEARS, A PROVEN MODEL OF SUCCESS

In 2004, while serving as chairman of the House Appropriations Foreign Operations Subcommittee, our subcommittee worked to pass—with strong bipartisan support, I might add—the legislation creating the Millennium Challenge Corporation. After the MCC came into being, our subcommittee provided the initial funding for its operations and ongoing appropriations in the years that followed. MCC represented a new approach to foreign assistance, with a radical departure from the way programs had been designed and countries designated for foreign aid assistance in the past. Not everyone in the executive branch or in the development community, nor even some of my colleagues on Capitol Hill, were confident of its success. It was designed with the singular mission of reducing poverty through economic growth in the world's poorest but relatively well-governed countries. Its objectives, governance, and authorities were clearly spelled out in legislation to accomplish this overarching development purpose. The MCC's model of assistance is focused on four sound principles:

(1) Selectivity in determining which countries to partner based on agreed-upon criteria—objectively measured and objectively applied;
(2) A business-like approach to choosing investments using well designed analyses of constraints to economic growth;
(3) A focus on country ownership through the consultation, development, and implementation processes of each compact; and
(4) A rigorous commitment to transparency and accountability from beginning to end of a country compact.

First and foremost, MCC partners must earn their place in MCC's pipeline by sharing values that are common to democratic societies. They must demonstrate a commitment to ruling justly, investing in their people, and supporting democratic rights. By demonstrating this commitment—sometimes over multiple years and often only after undertaking significant and politically difficult reforms—countries are then able to work with MCC to address identified constraints to economic growth. Incentivizing reform in partner countries is a crucial policy aim of the MCC.

I've followed the MCC's work closely from its inception, and over its decade-long existence, the MCC has demonstrated that its model works. MCC has invested over $10 billion in eligible partner countries and improved the lives of millions of people around the world. Eligibility for MCC's sizeable grants is determined by measuring a country's performance against independent, transparent, selection criteria. By working exclusively with those countries that demonstrate a commitment to good governance, the rule of law and economic freedom, MCC has had the multiplying effect of compelling low income countries—even those who do not currently partner with MCC—to reform institutions, change laws, and improve how they operate in order to try to qualify for MCC assistance.

And the effect is not just taking place overseas where we provide assistance. I have seen it impact our own U.S. government, where larger organizations, such as USAID, have incorporated many of MCC's core principles into their own business practices. Responsiveness to country priorities, open and transparent practices, rigorous evaluations, and evidence-driven learning and decisionmaking are becoming the norm for development agencies here and abroad—no longer the exception.

However, as we peer over the horizon to the next 10 years, I want to offer my own reflections on how the MCC can continue to stay on the cutting edge of development while remaining true to its original intent.

ACCENTUATE MCC'S STRENGTHS AND STAY TRUE TO MISSION

First, there will always be a temptation by policymakers in the executive branch and here in Congress to allow new priorities to interfere with the MCC's core values. The MCC should not allow itself to succumb to other considerations, strategic or otherwise, that are inconsistent with, or run counter to, MCC's fundamental approach. Long-term development requires focus and discipline. Bringing the 800 million people in the world who remain in the shadow of the worst poverty is an end in itself with its own strategic purpose. It cannot, and should not, be an instrument of day-to-day diplomatic engagement or set aside in order to respond to the political crisis of the day.

What has made the MCC successful has been its unwavering commitment to the principles upon which it was founded: democracy, rule of law, good governance, and transparency. These are principles deeply imbedded in the American value system. But they are also principles which peoples of other countries strive to incorporate into their own governing process. A desire for democratic decisionmaking, to have a government free of corruption, to be shielded by adherence to the rule of law—these are not exclusively American values.

In an effort to ensure public accountability, when the MCC was established it included in the founding legislation a private-sector component of the MCC's Board: four private-sector members appointed by the President of the United States with the advice and consent of the U.S. Senate. These members have worked in a bipartisan fashion in successive administrations to honor the MCC's mandate by maintaining the rightful focus on the MCC's development objectives, even when confronted with sometimes unrelated policy priorities and emergencies. Even when foreign policy issues directly involve MCC partner countries, the Board has worked together to prioritize and uphold MCC's mission.

Second, the MCC model has always been built on the idea of partnership, with developing countries setting the course for MCC engagement by identifying their own objectives and designing and implementing their own program. In fact, the legislation creating the MCC was deliberately designed to contain no earmarks for specific sectors or purposes, thus giving countries the political and policy flexibility to determine their own priorities. Over time, MCC has integrated a number of requisite steps to foster inclusiveness and accountability, including constraints-to-growth analysis, broad local consultation, economic rate of return assessments, and monitoring and evaluation plans. Facilitating a process for governments and communities to lead their development and be accountable for results should guide U.S. assistance policy. I am confident that with the passage of time we will find that one of the long term benefits of the MCC will prove to be its ability to strengthen the citizen-state compact so that governments are more responsive to the needs of the people our assistance is intended to help.

Third, the MCC has been a pioneer on transparency, publishing data elements from the start of a compact through to its completion. The MCC expects to soon add subnational location data and disaggregated results data. For its efforts, MCC has consistently ranked as one of the most transparent donor agencies in the world by the organization, "Publish What You Fund." This dogged adherence to openness ensures accountability to both U.S. taxpayers and citizens of partner countries.

MCC'S ROAD AHEAD: BUILDING ON A SOUND APPROACH

I applaud the MCC's interest in concurrent compact authority which would enable it to undertake regional investments in an effective and efficient manner. Concurrent compacts would allow the MCC authority to break up implementation of compact components between fiscal years. This would allow more time for compact development and due diligence, which in turn could yield more effective results. Such authority would provide more flexibility to the existing 5-year model employed by MCC, as compact completion could extend beyond 5 years on compacts approved by Congress for concurrent funding. Enactment of concurrent compact authority would also allow MCC to accelerate compact development and implementation, while ensuring adequate time for the more detailed, technical project development needed for complex projects.

In addition, the law that established the MCC explicitly provides the authority for the agency to negotiate coinvestment agreements with the private sector. Public-private partnerships will be necessary for the MCC to achieve its mission in an era of limited government resources. When the MCC was proposed by President George W. Bush in 2003, the stated goal was for the MCC to provide $5 billion in assistance per year. Yet, 10 years later, its annual budget is slightly less than $1 billion. The only practical way for the MCC to achieve transformational growth and poverty eradication is to leverage private sector investment alongside MCC compacts. Therefore, the MCC must incorporate the private sector from the beginning of compact development process to effectively utilize private resources alongside compact investments. The MCC must also be vigilant to ensure that its compact investments are designed to catalyze but never to replace or crowd out private-sector investment.

MORE WORK NEEDED: CORRUPTION AND INCOME CATEGORIES

MCC's Control of Corruption Indicator must be strengthened, allowing for greater distinction between those countries that are meeting the criteria and those that are not. Good governance does not equate to lack of corruption. Better data is needed for the corruption index so that the MCC can make discreet and realistic distinctions between countries that are really tackling corruption and those that are not. Without this we cannot prevent misuse of U.S. taxpayer dollars nor assure projects are actually helping those for whom they are designed.

The MCC should also take a closer look at the Low Income Country (LIC) and Lower Middle Income Country (LMIC) categories to ensure we are targeting the right set of countries with our assistance. MCC legislation requires that only 25 percent of MCC funds may be used for LMICs, and the MCC continues to use gross national income per capita as measured by the World Bank as the metric for determining income groups. But the world has changed since MCC first started to work. Nearly 2 billion people have been lifted from deep poverty, so the pool of countries at the economic bottom is—thankfully—shrinking. Congress needs to examine whether the 25 percent cap on funds for LMICs is appropriate in today's world and whether the World Bank's GNI measure is the most effective.

THE MCC LONG VIEW: CONTINUE TO INNOVATE BY TAKING SMART RISKS

Development is an inherently difficult, protracted, and risky business. The legislation my subcommittee helped to enact provided clear objectives, principles, and parameters, while giving MCC and its partners the flexibility to test new ideas and approaches in program areas, methods, and implementing structures. This kind of innovation is necessary to keep MCC at the forefront of development, but more importantly, for U.S. development efforts to be transformational and actually lead to sustainable outcomes.

I believe the MCC has at times shied away from experimentation due to the political risks associated with innovating. Oversight understandably tends to focus predominantly on where public funds are spent and whether they are being used properly. Assessing success or failure, however, should also take into account whether program objectives are achieved—or could be achieved more efficiently—while at the same time putting in place mechanisms for sufficient fiduciary responsibility.

One example would be to look more deeply into how we apply development assistance to increase the competence and accountability of partner countries' own systems and institutions. This is the only long-term pathway to sustainability, especially when, and after, assistance ends. A desire on the part of the U.S. Government to use capable country systems would provide a persuasive incentive for partners to improve and optimize their public financial management apparatus. This is the type of innovation the MCC and other U.S. agencies must explore more seriously if we are to reap better development rewards.

In conclusion, the MCC has shown itself to be a game changer in how we look at development assistance, engage partner countries, and achieve meaningful development outcomes that are measurable and clear. After 10 years, it is only appropriate for the MCC, and for Congress, to review the agency's track record and seek ways to strengthen the model so that it might do even more. In a time when limited fiscal resources can be devoted to development assistance, the American taxpayer will rightly insist that they be spent wisely and efficiently. Given the unique attributes of the MCC, and its performance-driven mission, I have no doubt it will remain up to this challenge.

Thank you, and I look forward to answering any questions you may have.

The CHAIRMAN. Thank you very much. Mr. Natsios.

STATEMENT OF HON. ANDREW S. NATSIOS, DIRECTOR OF THE SCOWCROFT INSTITUTE OF INTERNATIONAL AFFAIRS, AND EXECUTIVE PROFESSOR, THE BUSH SCHOOL OF GOVERNMENT AND PUBLIC SERVICE, TEXAS A&M UNIVERSITY, COLLEGE STATION, TEXAS

Mr. NATSIOS. Thank you very much, Senator Corker. Thank you very much for your invitation to speak. I have not been before your committee since, I think, I was envoy to Sudan.

The MCC makes three major contributions to the international development practice. First, the MCC relies on transparent and readily-available indicators to select countries for participation in compacts. This has several advantageous aspects to it, one of which is that countries know ahead of time what is expected.

Secondly, the MCC compiles the data it uses, these 20 indicators, and publishes it, and those scorecards are used even beyond the MCC. The business community looks at these scorecards to see where countries are. Thirdly, and most importantly, compacts are locally designed, driven, and carried out.

Now, I want to emphasize that perhaps the most important but least understood aspect of the strengths of the MCC are its decentralization. Our aid program, other than MCC, has become more and more centralized over the last 10 years. Carol Lancaster, former dean of the law school at Georgetown, said it was by stealth. This stealth takeover of USAID by the State Department and by the Office of Management and Budget's growing control in terms of demands for indicators for everything, and short timelines for projects.

The old USAID during the Cold War had 20-year projects. If you call someone to get your computer repaired, the person you get may come from India, and they probably were educated at an engineering school. There are 13 of these technical schools built by the Indian government and the U.S. aid program in the 1950's and 1960's.. USAID linked these 13 engineering schools in India with13 of the best U.S. Engineering Schools. This linkages program was very successful in building the capacity of the Indian Schools. Most Indians do not know that it was USAID (or its predecessor agencies) that built those schools . But it was the U.S. that did it.

The premiere engineering school in India was the one that linked with MIT for 20 years under these projects. USAID does not do 20 year projects anymore. The Agency stopped doing that a long time ago and instead went to 10-year projects, then to five-year projects. Many USAID career staff tell me now that because of the control that the State Department and OMB the Agency now reviews every project every year. Even though officially projects last five years, every year the overseers review everything, and if they need money for other initiatives, they shut down a project, and move the money somewhere else.

It is very destructive to the development process to have one-year projects. Someone in the administration privately described our aid program over both the Bush and Obama administrations in Afghanistan as 13 one-year projects. And that is one of the problems that has not been looked at, at all.

Professor Dan Honig at the Johns Hopkins School of Advanced International Studies did a detailed analysis of 8,000 aid projects from five or six aid agencies—e.g the World Bank, USAID, the British Aid Agency—and he looked at the degree of autonomy of local managers had versus highly centralized systems where everything has to be approved at the headquarters. And he found a significantly higher level of success in highly decentralized systems. USAID used to be the most decentralized aid agency in the world, and other development agencies were jealous because they could actually make decisions in the field without going to Wash- ington all the time. That has been reversed in the last 10 years, and it has damaged our development programs. The only holdout in the old system of decentralization is the MCC. That is not dis-cussed much, but in my view, it is extremely important.

The second issue I think that we need to look at is the issue of who we are competing with. China has an entirely new model of development cooperation. Actually it is not a new model. It is the model we used in the 50s and 60s. It was an infrastructure-based model for development. What has led to the 12 percent growth rates in China? Of course that rate has collapsed now, but for 20 years the focus was on infrastructure in China. Most of their development, in fact, was physical development. It was building, dams, bridges, ports, and highways, and rural roads.

We stopped doing those projects a long time ago. Congress and OMB argued these projects were too expensive, damaged the environment and had maintenance problems. It took too long to build the projects and maintain them, and the consequence of that is that many of the Western donors and the World Bank have gotten out of the infrastructure business. This has opened up the field to China, which is now filling the gap. Much of the MCC's spending is on infrastructure projects because that is what developing countries need and want.

The third question I would like to raise here is the relative independence of the MCC from the use of foreign aid for geostrategic purposes. Now, I was a diplomat for a year and a half. I know how important the USAID programs are to our national security. If the State Department or the Defense Department wishes to use foreign aid for very short-term strategic purposes, they have an account to do that. It is called the ESF (the Economic Security Fund) account. Congress appropriates money every year to that account. They should use that account, not the rest of our aid budget.

What the Defense and State Departments do in strategically important countries is use our regular aid budget and sometimes the MCC for diplomatic and national security purposes. This is inappropriate, even under Federal statute. I think it is on the edge of frankly being illegal sometimes when they do this. Several countries have been approved for compacts that were not eligible. The MCC staff strenuously opposed it. USAID also opposed it, but the State Department under pressure from the Defense Department, for strategic reasons, approved a couple of these countries. I do not want to go into the details here. I am happy to do it privately. There are national security interests at risk. I understand why they did it from a diplomatic standpoint. But these countries were well below the corruption index requirement under the MCC legislation.

I completely agree with Jim Kolbe's comments on the importance of separating the MCC from the strategic short-term interests of the United States. That is not the purpose of the program. It is clear in the statute that it was designed by the White House or the Congress for this purpose. If they need to make those kind of commitments, they should do it through the ESF account.

These are my comments. I endorse the program. I think it is very important. But I think we need to protect the MCC's original mandate in the original legislation.

[The prepared statement of Mr. Natsios follows:]

PREPARED STATEMENT OF ANDREW S. NATSIOS

Mr. Chairman, thank you for the opportunity to testify today on the strengths and weaknesses of the Millennium Challenge Corporation, and to propose some changes in the authorizing legislation.

The Millennium Challenge Corporation was created by President George W. Bush as major reform in the international aid system, where we would reward those countries that made significant strides to improve their governance, economic freedom and expand investments in their people. President Obama has continued White House support for the program which indicates that the MCC business model has strong bipartisan support. More than 10 years after the 102nd United States Congress passed the authorization for the MCC, we can take stock of its successes.

The MCC makes three major contributions to the international development practice. First, the MCC relies on transparent and readily available indicators to select countries for participation in compacts, which is advantageous in multiple ways— it makes the MCC effect possible, for one. Second, the MCC compiles the data it uses for selection in a scorecard of all twenty indicators, which it publishes for all countries for which is has data. This scorecard is now a valuable tool for private investors considering entry into a developing country. Third, and importantly, compacts are locally designed, driven and carried out with input from the MCC staff.

Local ownership of compacts is important because project success rates increase substantially when the management of projects is decentralized. Professor Dan Honig, at the John Hopkins School of Advanced International Studies, has shown a significantly higher success rate in aid projects where the local managers have a much higher degree of independence than those where management decisions are highly centralized. Over the past 10 years there has been a significant centralization of decisionmaking in U.S. Government aid program in the State Department which has compromised the integrity and success rates of these programs, given the findings of Honig's research. The MCC has the last hold out in the federal foreign aid system to this creeping centralization, but it too is at risk.

The reality is, of course, that within certain bounds, recipient countries (and project managers in the field) are much better suited to make crucial decisions about how projects should take shape. With increased local participation and local management, it is also more likely that projects are carried through till the end—both because the project was tailored to local needs, and because local officials will take ownership of the projects. Moreover, the local implementation authorities created when a compact is awarded contribute to building the capacity of governments in the recipient countries. Accordingly, locally driven compacts will tend to be more sustainable in the long run.

One success story that is worth mentioning is the George Walker Bush Highway in Ghana, which was built with funding from the MCA. The highway is an embodiment of Ghana's success in its efforts to rapidly modernize its economy and political system. The highway has substantially improved market access in regions of Ghana that had been relatively isolated from international markets.

After 10 years, we can conclude, with some assurance, that the MCC is a success story. We have certainly learned many lessons, but moving forward we should refine the MCC and not reform it.

In my testimony below are several suggested reforms to the MCC. The two most important improvements are the composition of the board—where the Secretary of State should not hold the chairmanship if we expect the MCC to live up to its mandate—and the use of the current corruption indicator, the purpose of which is more effectively carried out by the rule of law indicator.

Moreover, while the MCC is successful in its mandate, it is not an alternative to the United States Agency for International Development (USAID). The MCC is designed to only operate in the most ideal conditions—those where good governance, economic freedoms and investments in people have already been demonstrated. Much of USAID's work is specifically designed to operate under other and more challenging local conditions, as is necessary to fulfill its much broader mandate.

Strengthening the MCC is more important now than ever. The MCC compacts provide alternatives to Chinese loans and infrastructure development which do not encourage good governance or improved local capacity. The MCC has focused much of its funding on infrastructure, particularly in Africa, because that is what the people and leaders of the countries have chosen to focus their projects on. Donor government tend to appropriate money for sectors which are popular in wealthy countries, such as health, education, and the environment while what the developing countries need and want to build their economies are roads, bridges, and other infrastructure. When countries are left to make development decisions themselves, they prioritize these projects over social services because they know that we have forgotten that without economic growth and the tax revenues it generates, social services are unsustainable. Chinese aid is heavily focused on infrastructure and that is why it is so popular in the developing world. The MCC effectively rewards those countries that strive to achieve improvements for their citizens, but the relatively small budget of the MCC is dwarfed by China's efforts.

THE "MCC" EFFECT

A central and important difference between the MCC and other development agencies is the insistence on a commitment to good governance, economic freedom and investments in citizens in recipient countries. Potential recipient countries are well aware of the transparent, quantitative and objective thresholds that they must fulfil to qualify, which spurs reform and improvement in governance. Research by Bradley Parks and Zachary Rica (2013) found that policymakers in developing countries are sensitive to the eligibility criteria of the MCC, which acts as an external incentive to improve governance. The MCC effect is real, and it is a major contribution to the development community, where it will act as an example for other aid agencies. I saw the MCC effect at work while I served on the Board of Directors as USAID Administrator.

Studies show that improving governance, economic freedoms and social opportunities for citizens is important for economic development—an idea championed by Amartya Sen, who received a Nobel Prize for his work—which shows the complementarity of these different areas to economic growth, development in general and poverty alleviation in particular. The idea is firmly rooted in theory and evidence, and several major studies have come out detailing the relationship, including the report by the World Bank, "Assessing Aid—What Works, What Doesn't, and Why." The better countries score on these indicators, the more likely they are to success- fully turn an MCC compact into economic growth, and the more likely it is that the economic growth benefits those citizens in poverty. However, improving governance, economic freedoms and social opportunities is also an end in itself for the 20 indicators the MCC uses to measure this. In fact, many of the indicators are measures of fundamental human rights, such as access to primary education, property rights and the right to participate in government. The MCC effect is such that even before funds are committed to a compact, the United States makes a difference in the lives of millions, with the promise of rewarding those governments that pursue these rights and freedoms for their peoples.

Recognizing that reforms and improvements in governance, economic freedoms and social opportunities can be costly, the MCC supports countries that have shown commitment to improving governance, but do not yet qualify for full compacts, by way of 'threshold' programs that assist governments financially to fund reform and improvements. The difficulty with the threshold programs is they are so small in funding and scope that their impact is limited. One refinement of the MCC would be to approve fewer threshold programs with larger commitments of money for longer periods of time which would increase their effectiveness.

While there is little doubt that the MCC effect is real, it is very difficult to measure the magnitude of the effect. The Office of the Inspector General of USAID funded a quantitative study by Johnson, Goldstein-Plesser and Zajonc (2014) of the effect, which yielded no conclusive evidence, one way or the other. Other studies have attempted to find a measurable difference between those countries we would expect to be affected by the MCC, and those that are not, with more but still limited success. However, in all cases, the authors point out that these results should not lead us to think the effect does not exist, but rather to conclude that we cannot yet measure it.

In my own research ("The Clash of the Counter-Bureaucracy and Development" published by the Center for Global Development, in 2010),[1] I demonstrate how the focus on quantitative measures of success damages and distorts how we approach development because it ignores a central aspect of development theory—that those development programs that are most precisely and easily measured are the least transformational, and those programs that are most transformational are the least measurable.

This does not mean that we should stop attempting to estimate and measure our success, but instead that our overreliance on numbers and figures to evaluate development success is misleading and undermines good development practice. The OMB, the GAO, the IG, the State Department's Foreign Aid office, and Congressional oversight committees have forced both the MCC and USAID to collect massive amounts of program data which is never used by anyone and which does not actually demonstrate outcomes successfully. This entire system of aid oversight needs reform.

There are four distinct reasons why the MCC effect is difficult to measure. The first is simply that the tools we have available to do so are so crude that subtle, but important improvements in governance, economic freedom and social opportunities are too small for our tools to capture. The second issue is that many indicators that are used by the MCC on the scorecard, especially those relating to corruption and good governance (where the most important local reforms take place) are not appropriate for tracking change over time. Moreover, because the indicators are measured, collected and published by third parties (which is in other aspects a strength of the MCC indicators), a change in governance this year may not show up for a year or two, simply because measurement, preparation of the indicators, and publication, take time. But we also know from other research that many development programs display a time lag between the end of a program and the improvement in outcomes.

A third challenge is that the MCC is still a relatively small program, with a relatively modest budget. The threshold programs, which exist to help governments improve governance, economic freedom and social opportunities, by law accounts for less than 5 percent of the MCC's total budget. The current budget for the MCC is creating change, but we cannot expect transformational change—the profound shift

---

[1] http://www.cgdev.org/publication/clash-counter-bureaucracy-and-development

of indicators—without committing at a higher level over a longer time horizon. If we hope for the MCC to have a great impact by catalyzing reform, then the compacts must be larger in size. The MCC can accomplish this within existing appropriations by approving fewer, but larger, compacts.

A fourth, and important challenge is the long time horizon associated with the type of change we are working to incentivize. Investments in anticorruption this year, for example, will not substantially change the indicator the following year or two, even if the program is as successful as one could hope for. Many development outcomes, especially those relating to changes in governance, attitudes and business practices change slowly, and they are not always appropriately captured by quantitative indicators. Many of USAID's most successful governance projects showed results over a decade or two, not over months or years. As USAID has been gradually absorbed into the State Department, the length of development projects have become shorter and shorter, and that poses a significant threat to the efficiency and success rate of our foreign aid programs because there exists an inverse relationship between project length and project success. In other words, when projects are forced to work on a short time-horizon, development outcomes are adversely affected. During the cold war, aid programs covered timespans of 20 years, they gradually declined to 10 years, and while I served as USAID Administrator they declined to 5 years. Many aid projects today in practice last one year as they are constantly being reassessed as the State Department or OMB wants to free up money for some other diplomatic initiative.

Despite these measurement issues, it is still clear that the MCC effect is real. Passing the MCC's scorecard does not automatically lead to funding of a compact for the country, so the effect is more profound than reforms for the sake of securing funding. As a corollary to the MCC effect, passing the MCC's scorecard is an important signal to the private sector that looks to "passing" the scorecard as a seal of approval akin to the World Bank's "Cost of Doing Business Index." In the study by Bradley Parks and Zachary Rica (2013) at College of William and Mary, the MCC ranked as one of the three most influential external assessments of government.

If one relies on qualitative evidence instead, the MCC effect is even clearer. The MCC and others have provided testimony of instances where governments directly sought the MCC's guidance and assistance in overcoming governance obstacles, particularly with respect to corruption. Examples of a direct impact of MCC criteria range from Albania to Sierra Leone and Armenia. In Sierra Leone the government finally passed the scorecard in 2013 after years of reforms guided by the MCC and others.

It is important not to overstate the magnitude of the MCC effect, but it is a significant aspect of the MCC's success. So too is it important to recognize that the MCC effect is not the explicit goal of the MCC, which is poverty reduction through economic growth, but rather an additional outcome of the program beyond poverty alleviation.

THE COMPLEMENTARITY OF THE MCC AND USAID

The MCC is not an alternative to USAID, and it is crucial that the MCC is not seen as such. The MCC has a more limited scope, concentrated in countries where we would expect development programs to be the most successful because good governance, economic freedoms and investments in human capital contribute substantially to economic growth. The ownership and local project management, which is important to the MCC model, is likewise only possible because the countries that pass the threshold are much more likely to possess the capacity to manage a compact than countries that do not qualify. While the MCC's single mandate is to alleviate poverty through economic growth, many mandates that cannot be achieved with MCC's model fall to USAID.

Among those mandates which fall outside the mission of the MCC is the work of the U.S. Office of Foreign Disaster Assistance that provides humanitarian aid in complex emergencies such as conflict and famine, and the work of USAID's Office of Transition Initiatives, which supports U.S. foreign policy objectives by supporting political transitions and supporting democracy building. Additionally, USAID was an indispensable leader in the U.S. nation-building efforts in Afghanistan and Iraq, and it will continue to be important for their recovery as well as in global health programs.

The MCC and USAID are thus complementary institutions that can reinforce the other's work, but they carry out fundamentally different tasks within the development process. USAID often operates in unstable conditions, where good governance is absent or has collapsed and where economic freedoms are a distant dream. Often USAID works in those environments to save and protect life, to enable basic markets to function and to prevent situations from deteriorating. The MCC, by its legal mandate, only operates in stable conditions and where markets function relatively well and is thus not a substitute for USAID.

Even in the countries that pass the MCC scorecard and where the MCC can thus operate, USAID fills many other roles than those relating specifically to economic growth. A third of the U.S. Government's foreign aid budget (much of it administered by USAID) is focused on global health, specifically on the world-wide eradication or treatment of different diseases such as Polio, HIV/AIDS, Ebola, and Malaria. USAID's very successful trade capacity building, "World Bank Doing Business" reforms, and economic competitiveness programs by their nature require policy dialogue with local business leaders and technical assistance which the MCC is not designed to do. In fact, while the MCC funds the threshold programs to assist governments in improving governance, economic freedoms and social opportunities, it is most often USAID that is contracted to carry out those programs.

FOCUSING ON CORRUPTION

Of the twenty indicators on the MCC's scorecard, a single indicator reigns above the rest. Whereas countries must place higher than the median in half of the indicators to qualify, control of corruption is an indicator that a country must pass to qualify, no matter how good the average of the others indicators is. It is a difficult requirement, and rightly so, in recognition of how central corruption is to the economic, political and social maladies in poorly governed countries. We possess an abundance of evidence that corruption is bad for economic growth, bad for poverty alleviation and bad for political inclusiveness. President George W. Bush was the author of the requirement which he insisted be written into the legislation, and which has inspired anticorruption reforms and campaigns in several MCC candidate countries.

We should continue to place a high premium on reducing corruption, but we can refine the MCC's ability to use the hard indicator as a tool for selection, and for inducing change in countries that wish to qualify. The current indicators for corruption are largely "perception"-based, meaning that if those surveyed perceive a high prevalence of corruption, then the country will score poorly on the indicator.

Perception does affect economic behavior, but it is only a minor part of what the indicator is actually attempting to measure. Because corruption is hard to quantify and measure (most people don't advertise their own corruption), the indicator uses perception as a way to estimate the full level of corruption in a country. It is what scholars would call a proxy—the use of an indicator that can be measured to extrapolate about a phenomenon that cannot. However, the perception aspect of the indicator can have unintended consequences that work against what the President and Congress designed the MCC to achieve.

One of the tools USAID uses widely to combat corruption is increasing public awareness of corruption and its destructive consequences, and educating people about how it can be dealt with. In many countries corruption is viewed as a way of life and not an aberration of government, which is a major obstacle to effectively combating corruption. However, raising public awareness about corruption—so it can be detected, reported, deterred and sanctioned—will also tend to raise the perception of corruption because the public is increasingly made aware of its presence and negative effects, and that increase in perception—even though corruption has not increased—is detrimental to the MCC's work. Simply put, with the current indicator, those countries that effectively improve on corruption can simultaneously be penalized for their efforts.

The solution is simple because the contributions of the hard target in the corruption indicator can be achieved with another established measurement: the Rule of Law indicator. Rule of law captures corruption in government through multiple measures, ranging from the independence of the judiciary and agents of the law, the impartiality, independence and accountability of the police force, the protection against government overreach in expropriation and so forth. The hard target for corruption should be based on this indicator instead. However, moving the hard target from the corruption indicator to the rule of law indicator requires the approval of Congress in any future refinement of the legislation.

INDEPENDENCE

On the matter of MCC independence, it is crucial that this be strengthened. The main benefits of the MCC's approach—the transparent, indicator-based system that spurs the MCC effect—depend on the MCC's credibility in using indicators for selection. The President's wish that the MCC would provide a new, innovative and effective kind of aid, based on hard evidence, is derived in part from the MCC's transparent and predictable methods. Another central facet of the MCC's success—local ownership, design and implementation of compacts—is indelibly linked to the MCC's ability to create sustainable capacity in compact countries. Anything but evidence-based selection of the best projects would undermine the MCC's work and the best use of aid funds in the MCC model. Recall that the MCC's mandate already ensures that aid is spent in the interest of the United States by focusing only on those countries that already have significant levels of political and economic freedoms and invest in their people.

In general, the involvement of the State and Defense Departments in specific development and humanitarian aid decisions has undermined the effectiveness of our aid, for USAID and the MCC alike. We have to make a very clear decision about whether or not our foreign aid is a grand strategy tool that we wish to employ to reward or punish other countries when they either support our goals or oppose them, respectively. Foreign aid is often used for entirely contradictory purposes—sometimes development for the purposes of development or other times as a tool of diplomatic and national security strategy. Hans Morgenthau argued this in his now famous 1962 article, "A Political Theory of Foreign Aid," where he suggested aid was given as a form of legal bribery to induce a change of diplomatic behavior on the part of the a recipient of the aid. On the other hand, we can decide—as the President and a bipartisan Congress did when it authorized the MCC—that the purpose of our foreign aid is to create a stable, democratic, and resilient world around us, which ultimately more broadly supports our foreign policy in profound ways.

South Korea is an excellent example that demonstrates the power of good development. Over the course of 30 years, USAID spent about 6 billion dollars (in 1960's dollars) in development programs to support economic growth and basic public goods such as sanitation, schools and infrastructure, which ultimately support economic growth as well. With the help of U.S. Government aid, South Korea rose out of poverty to be a prosperous, democratic and stable ally that is indispensable to the United States in preserving peace in East Asia. South Korea is a strong and active partner that keeps North Korea in check. However, USAID's work in South Korea would not have been as successful if it had been used to support of shorter and more parochial diplomatic objectives of U.S. foreign policy.

Using aid as a bargaining chip might satisfy short term goals in some cases by buying the support of a warlord or important political faction, but it undermines the developmental use of aid to create prosperity and support the longer term interest of the United States. That should not come as a surprise: if aid allocation is not made based on the development potential, but instead based on political, short-term priorities, then our development funds will not be effective. In such cases, of which there are many, USAID is then criticized for the lack of results in suboptimal development programs that they are forced by the State and the Defense Department, and sometimes Congress, to design without regard for their development potential. In many cases these "development aid" funds are outright damaging our longer term goals. As USAID has been absorbed into the State Department, good development aid has become increasingly harder to do.

In fact, even the MCC is affected, despite the original intention of its mandate. As chairperson of the board, the Secretary of State has a disproportionate influence on compact decisions. Only one Secretary of State—Condoleezza Rice—shied away from making the MCC work for more parochial State Department objectives. She recognized that the independence of the MCC was one of its strongest attributes, even if the ultimate decision of the board did not align with her own preference. While it makes sense that the Department of State should be represented on the board, the Secretary of State should not hold the chairmanship. In fact, I would suggest an outside chairperson who does not hold public office as a statutory requirement. If the State Department wishes to reward an ally with aid for strategic purposes which is an important tool in a diplomats toolbox, they can use the Economic Security Fund account which was designed precisely for that purpose. I served on the U.S. delegation at the Hong Kong trade round in 2005 and watched to my dismay as USDA and State Department diplomats attempted to promise MCC compacts to countries for supporting the U.S. position in the negotiations on agriculture trade. I strenuously objected as the use of compacts for this purpose which in my view was an egregious violation of the intent and purpose of the MCC statute. These U.S. career officers backed down and the compacts were never promised.

Moreover, the intention of the President and the Congress of the United States was for the MCC to be entirely independent from political and strategic pressure, as was abundantly clear at the time of the MCC's authorization. When the State Department, or any other actor, affects compact or threshold decision outcomes, it is in violation of federal law and in violation of the original intentions of the MCC's founders. Several countries have been approved which clearly did not come close to meeting the indicators.

The independence of USAID and the MCC is imperative because developing countries put faith in the advice our development agencies offer. In many countries our aid agencies are well regarded and trusted, which occasionally leads aid workers having highly developed and influential relationships with government ministries and civil society organizations. If the perception among recipients is that our development programs are designed to serve U.S. short term strategy in mind, the work of USAID and the MCC will be made more difficult, even in the best designed projects.

I spent a while as a United States diplomat, so I have the utmost admiration for the State Department's work in diplomacy. In my view, our diplomats are among the best in the world. They should leave the management of aid development programs to development professionals in USAID and the MCC.

OPERATING IN FRAGILE STATES

The MCC faces challenges in countries where governance, economic freedoms and social opportunities are suboptimal. In a few cases this fragility led to the early termination or suspension of compacts because the relevant indicators fell. While that is regrettable, I would argue that the termination and suspension of these compacts should be looked at as a success for the MCC. While the MCC could certainly improve its ability to help countries progress in governance, economic freedoms and social opportunities, as could all other aid agencies in the world, terminating the compact is not a symbol of failure but evidence of success in the rigor and discipline of the process. It is a victory for those countries that work hard to make real, sustainable improvements in their indicators.

If entry into a compact is based on a certain level of indicators that must be achieved, then those levels should be enforced after the compact has begun as well. Otherwise the improvement in the indicators is insincere; countries could improve to qualify, knowing that they could simply reverse reforms once the compact is granted. By enforcing the levels of the indicators after a compact is initiated, the MCC prevents opportunistic behavior. Enforcement is thus paramount to the MCC's mission of sustainable improvements in governance, economic freedoms and social opportunities.

CONCURRENT AND REGIONAL COMPACTS

A significant impediment to economic development is a lack of intraregional infrastructure and cooperation. One particular category of countries—those that are landlocked—depend almost entirely on their connection with neighbors for access to the rest of the world, as demonstrated by Paul Collier in his seminal book, "The Bottom Billion." In fact, the infrastructure projects including airports for landlocked countries is their connection to the global economy. Even for those with global market access, development tends to be closely related to the development of neighboring countries. Concurrent compacts would enable the MCC to operate in this crucial area of development, which is necessary for long run sustainable development in many areas, particularly in Africa.

A crucial aspect of economic development in many countries is market access: the greater a country's access, and the wider the market for its products for export, the more trade country a country can sustain. Intercountry trade improvements in particular can be beneficial to economic growth. If the regional compacts are carried out appropriately, the benefits that accrue are even beyond economic growth. With better connectivity, and cooperation in a compact, the MCC will assist in building bridges—literal and figurative—that will enable governments to increase cooperation in many areas, including security, politics, border control and epidemiological control, all of which are in the interest of the regions and the United States of America alike.

A regional compact would, of course, be a new type of challenge for the MCC. Whereas a traditional compact only has one qualifying government, regional compacts would by definition have more, and all governments should pass the thresholds for the regional compacts to be implemented. It also requires significant coordination between the administrating bodies set up in each country to handle the Millennium Challenge Accounts. While these factors would complicate the approval process, it would not make it impossible for regional compacts to be approved and managed.

THE PERFORMANCE INDICATORS

These indicators are an important aspect of the work the MCC does, and a fundamental requirement for the MCC effect. There are several aspects of the indicators that are worth considering, both to refine how they are used in the future and to understand their limitations.

Importantly, the indicators are used as a transparent and easily identifiable cutoff for eligibility. In theory, this means that compacts are only awarded to those countries truly committed to good governance, economic freedoms, and social opportunities. It also means that countries have tangible goals they can work toward. Finally, the aggregate of the indicators—the MCC scorecards, which the MCC publishes for all countries that fall in the income categories every year—is also used by private and public actors alike to gauge how well a country performs in governance, economic freedoms, and social opportunities.

As a whole, the general level across all indicators will provide an insight into country performance in these aspects. Once we look at individual indicators, however, it becomes more troublesome to gauge the current conditions, because some of the indicators simply are not precise enough. This lack of precision does not stem from a lack of effort to measure the indicators well, but rather from a lack of data and, more importantly, from the fact that many of these indicators are trying to capture things that are very difficult to quantify. Judging a country's performance, and especially comparing the performance between countries, based on a single indicator, is unwise.

Consequently, the indicators are only useful for the MCC's purposes as a grouping of indicators, the total of which forms the scorecard. Refinements can surely be made to the specific indicators used, but as a whole, the MCC's use of the indicators is in line with the original intention of the President and the Congress. Our biggest contribution to the MCC here would be to encourage the MCC to upgrade to new measures as they become available, but in a transparent and timely manner. For the corruption indicator however, congressional approval is necessary.

The trouble comes when the indicators are used for other purposes than meeting the qualification threshold. Because the indicators are as crude as they are on their own, measuring the contribution of a threshold program for example—those designed to help countries in areas where they struggle—is difficult. What would be even worse is if we were to judge a compact based on whether it improved the indicators, because that is not the purpose of the compact—its purpose to is create economic growth and poverty alleviation. The indicators simply are not appropriate for evaluating the outcomes of programs, and they were never intended to be by the President and the Congress.

Moreover, the use of the indicators as a measure of the success of any development program is problematic. Beyond the timelag in measurement mentioned above, another and much more important timelag exists. To put it simply: development takes time. Attempting to quantify the success of programs in the next fiscal year is often nonsensical. In the case of South Korea, USAID helped lay the foundation that eventually enabled the South Korean economy to soar; the true extent of the benefits from USAID programs in South Korea were not known for at least two decades. With respect to governance and social opportunities in particular, perceptions and attitudes are among the major impediments to improvements, but perceptions and attitudes take a long time to change. Even where the MCC provides the tools for positive change, much of the benefit will not materialize for years.

A related issue pertains to the difference between output and outcomes in development. Output is oftentimes easy to measure: how many miles of road built, how many farmers trained, how many village councils established? However, what we ultimately want to know—what we term outcomes—is whether the road improved market access and reduced poverty, whether the farmers that were trained translated their training into improved crop yields or whether the village council were in fact inclusive and effective at using their mandate. Measuring the output does not guaranty a good outcome—nor does the absence of outputs mean that there cannot be successful outcomes. The overmeasuring of development thus yields little useful information and instead creates a significant amount of paperwork that serves no good purpose.

The MCC began with 17 indicators, and three more have since been added to the MCC's scorecard. It is hard to disagree with the indicators, either because they are morally important, or because we believe a new indicator is connected to economic growth. If we know the phenomenon that the indicator measures is important to economic growth, why should we not include it on the scorecard? The answer is again that the fixation on measurement is hurting the MCC's ability to carry out good compacts, and it also causes undue stress on the governments vying for a compact. Because the scorecard should be read as a whole and not as individual indicators, adding more indicators does not necessarily improve compact selection—it does, however, mean that potential recipients have to spread their already sparse government capacity to more indicators. This dilutes the efforts that governments are able to expend on individual areas, hurting progress. Most developing countries have limited capacity and weak institutions—even the ones which rank high in the indicators—which means their capacity to reform and make improvements in their countries have limitations. Piling one indicator on top of another will overwhelm their capacity to focus their efforts on a few reforms of the greatest significance. And, it creates a greater burden on MCC to compile and publish the scorecards with a greater number of indicators.

Without arguing that any specific indicators are unimportant to economic growth, we should reduce the amount of indicators on the scorecard (or at least freeze the number of the indicators at their present level) to improve the effectiveness of the scorecard on governments' behaviors and to reduce the adverse effects overmeasurement will have on potential recipients.

The MCC's reliance on a certain level of several indicators has led some observers to be concerned with the "conditionality" of MCC compacts, because conditionality was the main culprit behind the failure of much aid spending from the World Bank and other agencies in the 1980s and 1990s. However, the conditionality of the MCC is fundamentally different in several ways.

First, MCC conditionality takes place before compact-signing and without guarantees that a compact will be awarded, by excluding those countries that do not meet the requirements for application. Applying for a compact and moving towards the indicator levels is entirely voluntary—if a country does not find it in its own interest to enact the reforms necessary, it is not adversely affected, except by forgoing the potential funding.

In that same vein, the MCC's conditionality does not force specific policy prescriptions on countries. The MCC's conditionality is an "end goal" of a certain level in the indicators, as opposed to specific methods for reaching that goal. The World Bank prescribes specific (and sometimes inappropriate) policies that countries are forced to follow, but for the MCC indicators, it is largely up to countries to decide how to improve the indicators in ways which are most compatible with local circumstances.

Moreover, World Bank (and International Monetary Fund) conditionality in the 1980s and 1990s was often enforced for countries eligible for loans without which the recipient governments could not function, such as loans to sustain basic public goods or loans to help stabilize a country's currency during a time of crisis. Countries had very few choices but to accept the conditions, since without the loans and grants, the situation could deteriorate past a point of no return. In practice countries would agree to a laundry list of World Bank reforms which they would not end up implementing. In the case of the MCC, compacts cannot be held ransom in the same way, because they are designed to be above and beyond other efforts by USAID, the World Bank and other aid agencies, and because the compacts are not designed to sustain governments, but rather to create economic growth and reduce poverty.

In conclusion, the MCC has demonstrated success in achieving President Bush and the Congress' original aspirational goals of the authorizing legislation, but the legislation can be refined with some of proposed amendments suggested in this testimony. Thank you for the opportunity to speak today.

The CHAIRMAN. Thank you. Thank you very much.

Dr. Birdsall.

If I could just, so we do not leave that hanging, we are going to want to meet with you privately to ascertain whether what you just said relative to some of the things that may be happening at MCC and USAID are occurring. We want to set that meeting up, and Senator Cardin and I both will attend that, okay? Thank you.

STATEMENT OF NANCY BIRDSALL, PH.D., PRESIDENT, CENTER FOR GLOBAL DEVELOPMENT, WASHINGTON, DC

Dr. BIRDSALL. Chairman Corker, Ranking Member Cardin, members of the committee, thank you for this timely hearing. I am very privileged to have the chance to testify.

When MCC was created by the Bush administration, it was a bold bipartisan experiment, as we have heard, consistent with American values and foreign policy objectives. The idea was to support countries where the need is great and where foreign aid is most likely to be effective.

What is equally important, as we have heard, about the Agency is that over the last decade, MCC has set the standard in the aid community in other ways: using evidence to guide decisionmaking, focusing on results, adhering (as Congressman Kolbe said), doggedly to transparency, and partnering with countries in a way that ensures that countries take the lead in their own development. In quantitative assessments by my organization and the Brookings Institution, MCC has consistently scored near the top of more than 150 aid agencies around the world on aid effectiveness measures.

Today I want to focus on two areas where congressional action is needed to allow MCC to continue to build on its record of success, and two areas where continued support from Congress will help the Agency deliver even more of a development impact. And I will close with a plea to Congress about how to help USAID move in the direction by applying some lessons—the lessons learned from MCC.

First, regional compacts, which we have heard much about. I recommend that Congress authorize MCC to undertake a pilot project at the regional level with separate and additional funds above its country-based compact funds. Why? As you have heard, MCC has been active on the African continent, especially on major infrastructure investments, like roads and power. But with 54 small economies, the region's market is highly fragmented. The economic future for Africa is, therefore, in the kind of cross-border investments in Africa that you could compare to what the U.S. did during the Eisenhower administration with the interstate highway system.

Cross-border power projects in West Africa are probably the biggest impact opportunity for MCC right now. But the experience of the World Bank and the multilateral development banks on regional projects involving two or more countries, the experience is it is really hard to do. Negotiations are far more complex and take longer, and transactions costs and administrative costs are higher than with single country projects.

The point, however, is that MCC has two big advantages over the multilateral development banks. It has grant financing and the confidence that the U.S. government and U.S. businesses are involved in these projects. That is an asset, as Dana Hyde said. I am, therefore, pleased that Congress is considering concurrent compact authority for MCC. Without concurrent authority, there is little incentive for the Agency and little incentive for countries that are eligible to go regional despite the huge potential returns.

Second, the issue of country candidacy. The MCC mandate is to focus on poor countries, itself a good idea, below currently GNI per capita of just over $4,000. More fundamentally, I think it is to work with responsible governments in countries with a lot of poor people to help them grow into middle class societies, where the middle class eventually helps entrench and sustain responsible government without outside support.

The problem is that the current cutoff leaves out still poor countries that in every other respect would qualify for MCC compacts, and where the vast number of people live well below the United States poverty line, well short of what we would call even lower middle class. Consider Tunisia, a struggling democracy in a difficult region where most people live well below the U.S. poverty line, or Mongolia, which at the moment is at risk of losing a second compact because its per capita income GNI has risen, where most people are still poor and poorly educated, but where GNI is above the cutoff slightly because of recent foreign investment in its mining sector. U.S. support can help build a good government there— it can help a good government there, create the institutions, and make the investments that are still needed desperately on roads, schools, et cetera, that will spread that wealth to its people. But it will take time, in effect, building a middle class society. So I recommend that Congress ask the MCC to explore other measures to define country candidacy in terms of need that are more sensible reflections of a country's long-run needs.

Now, I want to go to two issues where Congress can encourage even greater MCC impact. One is a focus on funding measureable, verified development outcomes. I recommend that Congress encourage MCC's ongoing efforts to pilot what we call pay for performance approaches, like cash on delivery aid and development impact bonds.

With this approach, U.S. taxpayer money goes out the door only when development outcomes are achieved, like the number of additional households with affordable electricity access, not just when new—not just paying for new power lines, but paying for the outcome that we want of access to electricity. This kind of approach definitely creates greater country ownership and accountability of the kind that MCC has pushed on so effectively.

The second issue where Congress can help with its support is the idea of subsequent compact, second-round compacts. I recommend Congress continue to allow MCC to enter into subsequent compacts. Development simply does not happen in five years even with the most successful partnership. Subsequent compacts should not be automatic. MCC should have the discretion to enter into subsequent compacts where warranted.

Finally, let me close by encouraging Congress to take the MCC ethos beyond MCC. MCC has benefited from the start with the clear mandate to focus on aid effectiveness. USAID in contrast is burdened after over 50 years with an accumulation of congressional earmarks by country and sector, as well as other directives. I recommend Congress ask USAID to prepare a review of the directives and informal mandates that reduce its flexibility and undermine its ability—the ability of its excellent staff to maximize the impact of American taxpayers' foreign aid dollars.

Thank you very much.

[The prepared statement of Dr. Birdsall follows:]

PREPARED STATEMENT OF NANCY BIRDSALL[1]

Chairman Corker, Ranking Member Cardin, and members of the Committee, thank you for the opportunity to testify on the Millennium Challenge Corporation, a small but critical agency when it comes to U.S. efforts to reduce poverty and promote economic growth abroad. I am honored to be here and very pleased the Committee is holding this hearing.

My name is Nancy Birdsall and I am the president of the Center for Global Development, an independent, non-partisan think tank headquartered here in Washington, DC. CGD conducts research and produces analytical outputs aimed at improving the policies and actions of rich countries, including the United States, that affect developing countries.

The Center has been closely watching MCC from the agency's inception. And since MCC celebrated its tenth year anniversary just last year, this seems a fitting moment to reflect on its record and consider its future.

MCC was a bold experiment when it was created by President George W. Bush in 2004. The concept was simple: channel U.S. taxpayer money to poor countries that have responsible governments and sensible policies—those that encourage private sector activity, invest in schooling and health, fight corruption, and support democratic rights. This is consistent with American values and foreign policy objectives. Evidence suggests that these are the countries where foreign aid is most likely to make a difference by encouraging the policy changes that support longrun, sustained, poverty-reducing growth.

MCC's approach to delivering foreign assistance has set a standard for aid agencies around the world. It uses evidence to guide decisionmaking; it focuses on achieving and measuring results, evaluating the vast majority of its programs; it gives partner countries the lead role in identifying and implementing its investments; and, overarching all this, it is among the most transparent donors worldwide. In quantitative assessments of the efficiency and effectiveness of more than 100 global aid agencies conducted by the Center of Global Development with the Brookings Institution, MCC consistently scores near the top of aid agencies worldwide on a set of aid effectiveness measures.[2]

Today, I will focus on two areas where congressional action is needed to allow MCC to build on its strong record of success and two areas where continued support from Congress will help the agency deliver even more development impact. I will close with a plea for Congress to help other U.S. agencies apply lessons learned from the MCC.

(1) REGIONAL COMPACTS

Congress should authorize concurrent compact authority, and encourage MCC to pursue a regional pilot project with separate and additional funds above its country-based compact funds. Since regional projects bring an extra set of challenges, I recommend the agency start with a single pilot project accompanied by an independent review.

MCC has a strong record with road and power projects in bilateral compacts, but in regions like sub-Saharan Africa with many small economies and highly fragmented markets, some of the highest-return, growth-spurring investments only result from facilitating regional connections. In the U.S. context, for example, the Eisenhower Interstate Highway System was a federal initiative that linked people and markets across states—which no single State could have managed or would have financed.

To date, MCC has not been able to help eligible countries benefit from these kinds of returns because neighboring countries are rarely at the same stage of compact development at the same time; one country often has a compact underway by the time its neighbor is eligible. Concurrent compact authority (making countries eligible for a regional compact concurrent with a country compact covering some or all of the same period) offers a relatively simple fix to this shortcoming in the current MCC mandate.

Lack of this authority has impeded MCC's ability to encourage the necessary and often complicated negotiations between or among countries that is central to the planning and design of a cross-border investment—particularly since governments will generally choose to move expeditiously to lock in a national compact, rather than risk the more complicated, if higher-return, potential of a regional deal.

Outside funders do not have adequate incentives to work with countries to develop cross-border, regional projects despite their high returns. The multilateral development banks' (MDBs) still-limited experience explains why. With more than one partner country involved, negotiations are complex and upfront transaction costs mount quickly. The projects have long planning and implementation periods, and require strong and continuous implementation support.[3] Even so, successes are possible, as demonstrated by the Ethiopia-Kenya Interconnection energy project, supported by the African Development Bank and the SIEPAC power grid in Central America, supported by the Inter-American Development Bank.[4]

MCC has at least two advantages over other funders of large, cross-border investments in low-income countries. First, its grant financing eliminates the need to agree on the allocation of a repayment burden among beneficiary countries. Second, MCC's work on energy projects under the Power Africa umbrella indicates that the backing of the U.S. Government is a powerful force in generating confidence on the part of both private investors and partner governments in "getting to yes" on a complex investment deal.

It's easy to think about how regional engagement might be beneficial in the context of electricity. The logic of a shared grid across borders is clear. To work, countries involved need to commit to a strong regulatory and financial structure outside the auspices of a single government for power trading and pricing.[5] Grant money can play an important role in supporting upfront technical work and provide comfort to private investors in the guarantee of purchasing power agreements.

As many of you have recognized with your support of the Electrify Africa bill, reliable, affordable energy access is a massive constraint to growth in sub-Saharan Africa and elsewhere. A future regional power project covering Liberia, Cote d'Ivoire, and Ghana might be one promising pilot, for instance. MCC already has considerable experience with power under Power Africa and regional power investments in West and Southern Africa show potential.[6]

(2) A MORE SENSIBLE MEASURE OF NEED FOR COUNTRY CANDIDACY

Congress should allow MCC to explore whether an alternative measure of need to Gross National Income per capita (GNI) could produce a candidate pool that better reflects the significant poverty and development need in potential partner countries; one option is median daily consumption per person.[7]

As set out in the agency's authorizing legislation, only countries with a GNI below $4,125 (for FY2016) comprise the starting candidate pool for MCC engagement. Millions of people who are poor by any reasonable standard live in countries above this cutoff; and many countries above that level, despite good governance today, are not yet on a secure trajectory of sustained growth. American taxpayers want to support building middle class, democratic societies in the developing world, in which good government emerges and persists as income-secure taxpayers have the wherewithal to hold their governments accountable.[8] Many countries with GNI per capita above $4,125 are not yet middle class societies.[9] Consider Tunisia, a struggling democracy where per capita GNI is above MCC's cutoff. Yet one half of its population survives on less than $8 a day (Tunisia's median consumption level), compared to median (income) in the United States more than 10 times higher at over $50 per person a day.[10] The democratic government of Tunisia needs support if it is to stay on a trajectory of sustained, broad-based growth in a difficult region. Or Mongolia, also with median consumption of about $8, whose GNI per capita exceeds MCC's cutoff principally because of high foreign investment in its mining sectors, especially coal, copper, and gold. In Mongolia, it will take years to create the institutions and make the investments in health, education, roads, and energy that will bring the benefits of its newfound wealth to all of its people.

No single measure is perfect. Median consumption or income can be low because of a high concentration of income at the top of the distribution. But a country with low median income where corruption or tax or other policies fail to address high inequality would not be eligible for an MCC compact given the standards embedded in the MCC scorecard. Were MCC to adopt a measure like median income as a determinant of candidacy, the agency should consider investment grade and restrict partnerships with certain investment grade countries. Where the use of its grant resources is appropriate, MCC could target its funds to crowding in private investment.

(3) FOCUS ON FUNDING MEASURABLE, VERIFIED DEVELOPMENT OUTCOMES

Congress should support MCC in its ongoing efforts to pilot pay-for-performance approaches, such as Cash on Delivery Aid. These are agreements, developed by my colleagues and me at the Center for Global Development, in which donor agencies pay a partner country for the delivery of independently measurable and verified preagreed outcomes, like the number of additional households with affordable electricity access or average gains in learning of 10-year olds, rather than inputs such as new power lines or schools built.

Another approach—one which MCC is also exploring—is Development Impact Bonds (DIBs), also developed in part by the Center for Global Development. DIBs are also an outcomes-based approach in which private investors are invited to finance investments up front and are repaid if and when measurable results are verified. Given limited U.S. assistance dollars, this leveraging of private sector impact investors should be particularly welcome. Other donors have begun to experiment with pay-for-performance schemes—including the World Bank (Program-for-Results) and the UK's Department for International Development.

Pay-for-performance schemes fit well with many aspects of MCC's model. They promote greater country ownership and encourage innovation by providing partner governments with increased flexibility to find the best ways, within their own local context, to achieve agreed-upon targets. The approach is particularly useful where countries need to implement politically or bureaucratically difficult reforms if expected results or outcomes are to be gained. Political and institutional reforms are difficult to measure. It is most effective for countries to undertake them because doing so is key to increasing, for example, energy access or raising agricultural productivity or reducing waiting time for ships and trucks at ports and borders.

MCC has positioned itself on the cutting edge of thinking about results; to remain there it should push forward in its exploration of some of these new ways to link payments to outcomes.

(4) MORE IMPACTFUL PARTNERSHIPS THROUGH SUBSEQUENT COMPACTS

Congress should continue to allow MCC to enter into subsequent compacts. Development simply does not happen in 5 years, even with the most successful country partnership.

MCC was set up to work with well-governed developing countries. But development is a long-term project. It took Korea, one of the world's fastest growing countries in the 1960s and 1970s, something like 30 years to become what it is today: a middle class democracy. Tanzania (which is currently eligible for a second compact) would have needed to increase its per capita income by over 900 percent—over 50 percent per year—during the course of its first compact to reach upper-middle income status. More to the point, subsequent compacts can also capitalize on institutionalized relationships and lessons learned.

MCC's strict, 5-year compact timeline is a feature that sets it apart from other U.S. Government agencies. But the importance of the timeline is in its application to each compact—providing an incentive for timely implementation and forcing reassessment of continued engagement—not to MCC's overall relationship with a country. Second compacts (and potentially beyond) should not be automatic; but where warranted, a longer relationship should be welcomed.

(5) TAKING MCC BEYOND MCC

Congress should help other U.S. development agencies rise to the standard that MCC has set.

USAID and the State Department, which together control three quarters of U.S. foreign assistance dollars, should—for far more of their portfolio[11]—clearly demonstrate value for money, apply greater country selectivity, give partner countries more responsibility for identifying and managing aid investments, and further their commitment to transparency and rigorous evaluation.

This is easier said than done. MCC benefited from a fresh start as a new agency 12 years ago, and many of the features that have contributed to its excellence had been learned over many years in the aid community, and were hard-wired into MCC's culture and mandate from its inception. Compared to USAID, which is burdened with an accumulation over many decades of congressional directives on spending by country and sector as well as others, MCC has the flexibility to make reasonable demands on partner countries, to work with them on their own priorities, and to target results-focused investments (though still with appropriate oversight and quality controls).[12]

Congress must be a willing partner for a meaningful shift to take place throughout the U.S. development apparatus. A review of the external constraints that prevent USAID from exercising greater flexibility would be a good start toward building on the lessons of MCC. I also recommend that Congress request a comprehensive review of directives and informal mandates that constrain USAID and undermine key principles of aid effectiveness.[13]

CONCLUSION

In conclusion, I hope that Congress will continue its strong bipartisan support for MCC and encourage the agency to continue to adhere to its model. But I also urge Congress to push MCC to explore innovations within its model that would allow the agency to have even greater impact.

Notes

[1] Biography and CV: http://www.cgdev.org/expert/nancy-birdsall.

[2] Nancy Birdsall and Homi Kharas. "The Quality of Official Development Assistance (QuODA)." Washington, DC: Brookings Institution and Center for Global Development, 2014.

[3] World Bank. (2013)."Issues Remaining from the IDA16 Mid-Term Review." IDA Resource Mobilization Department Concessional Finance and Global Partnerships. Washington, DC: World Bank.

[4] The Kenya-Ethiopia energy project supports a 1,068 km transmission line from Ethiopia to Kenya and focuses on cost effective and clean energy sources.

[5] World Bank. (2008). Building Regional Power Pools: A Toolkit. Washington, DC: World Bank.

[6] The Southern Africa and West African Power Pools are examples.

[7] Data on median consumption or income is now available for more than 100 countries as a result of more frequent household surveys in the developing world. http://iresearch.worldbank.org/PovcalNet/index.htm?0,3

[8] Nancy Birdsall, "Does the Rise of the Middle Class Lock in Good Government in the Developing World?". European Journal of Development Research 27, 217–229 (April 2015).

[9] Nancy Birdsall, Nora Lustig and Christian Meyer, The Strugglers: The New Poor in Latin America?, World Development, Volume 60, August 2014, Pages 132–146, ISSN 0305-750X, http://dx.doi.org/10.1016/j.worlddev.2014.03.019.

[10] This is a rough estimate; median household income in the U.S. is about $50,000. At 2.5 people per household, per person median is about $20,000, or over $50 a day, http://www.census.gov/quickfacts/table/PST045214/00. Median consumption will be somewhat lower.

[11] MCC's set of standard practices is not systematically appropriate for all U.S. foreign assistance objectives and programs. USAID has important responsibility for emergency relief and humanitarian aid in many countries that would not be eligible for MCC support. In countries that are eligible, some efforts, like expanding the use of constraints analysis, a commitment made in the 2015 Quadrennial Diplomacy and Development Review, are more relevant for growth-focused programming. However, other aspects, such as cost-benefit-effectiveness analysis, country participation, evaluation, and transparency, can be applied more broadly, and across sectors and initiatives.

[12] Andrew Natsios, for example, also complains of the effects of the counter-bureaucracy of inspector generals that have increased risk aversion at USAID. See "The Clash of the Counter-bureaucracy and Development," Washington, DC: Center for Global Development, 2010.

[13] For one example of how such a review might be structured, see, Casey Dunning and Ben Leo. "Making USAID Fit for Purpose: A Proposal for a Top-to-Bottom Program Review." White House and the World. Washington, DC: Center for Global Development, 2015.

Senator CARDIN [presiding]. Thank you all for your testimony. Senator Corker has gone to vote. There is a vote on right now. I am going to ask questions for the record, so I will pass. I will want to follow up on the issue Mr. Natsios raised on the objectivity of decisionmaking and, Congressman Kolbe, on your point about how we can improve the corruption efforts—anticorruption efforts by MCC.

Senator Perdue.

Senator PERDUE. I will be very brief. We have to go make this vote. Thank you for your testimony and your work. As I mentioned to the earlier panel, I am concerned about the fact that because 40 percent of the money we have spent in the last seven years is borrowed, we have borrowed some $50 billion to support our USAID and our MCC work over the last just seven years alone.

And so, Congressman, I applaud what you guys did. It is funny how fast 10 years goes by. In that period of time, the earlier testimony was that of the programs that we have done, some 58 are averaging about 16 percent return versus the 10 percent threshold. In that period of time, though, there are some 21 projects that were done without having met the threshold for internal rate of return or the benefit cost analysis was not even calculated. And in addition, there were two specific projects where it looks like there was undue influence for strategic reasons for approval for a project without MCC or without MCC doing a benefit cost analysis.

So my question goes back to the original thinking. Given that over that period of time we spent—of a billion dollars a year, we spent $100 million on our own overhead in managing that, which means in the last 10 years we spent a billion dollars in overhead that did not help—did not go to any direct help. What is the—what

was the original thinking, and how was that debate won with regard to why MCC versus charging a part of USAID to focus on
eliminating poverty through economic growth?

Mr. KOLBE. Well, I will take a stab at it. I am sure Mr. Natsios
will also have an answer. I think the—first of all, I want to say
that I do disagree a little bit with the CEO, Ms. Hyde, in saying
that there has never been any pressure on MCC. That is not true.
There has been pressure from the get-go during the Bush administration as well as ongoing, and I think it is a natural thing that
the State Department and others are going to say, but, you know,
we have some strategic interests.

Senator PERDUE. But do we not have to protect——

Mr. KOLBE. That is what we need to do is—what the role of Congress is to make sure that it is protected from doing that. And I
think the outside independent private sector board members have
been the critical factor in making sure that happens.

Senator PERDUE. Can I ask you another question? I do not want
to get you off that line of answer, but the fact that the board reports directly to the Secretary.

Mr. KOLBE. He is chairman of the board.

Senator PERDUE. He is chairman, so that means that——

Mr. KOLBE. Yes.

Senator PERDUE [continuing]. There is no undersecretary or as-
sistant secretary that has responsibility for MCC. Is that correct?

Mr. KOLBE. That is correct.

Senator PERDUE. Is that working out in your mind in terms of
operational review and maintaining that independence?

Mr. KOLBE. I think it has worked as best that it can. I mean,
I guess you could think of other places that it might report, but I
think it is logical that the Secretary of State be the chairman of
it. And I think the fact that it has a board that includes several
agencies plus the four outside members, I think has been critical
to maintaining the independence of the board.

So I think by and large I would agree with Ms. Hyde that it has
been successful in resisting, for the most part, that pressure, not all
of it, but for the most part it has been successful in doing that. To go
to the thrust of your original question, the idea of it at the time we
created it was that USAID had a different mission, and this was—
the idea here was to work with countries that had a commitment to
governance, to good governance, and focus solely on that so that they
met objective criteria. And I can remember from the day we passed
that legislation, a line of ambassadors outside my door lining up to
say how do we get in. How are we going to get into this? And I would
say it is not up to me. I am not going to get you into it. It is going to
be your meeting these criteria that
is going to do it.

So I think it has been successful in that sense.

Senator PERDUE. Thank you. Mr. Natsios?

Mr. NATSIOS. USAID was deeply involved in the initial drafting.
In the original conception of this, USAID was supposed to run it,
and there were disputes among the White House staff we were
working with about who should run the MCC. I do not want to go
into it all. The President actually twice told his staff he did not

want to have two foreign aid agencies, and he did not understand why the staff kept insisting.

Senator PERDUE. Well, the question is what should we do? What is the best use of the money?

Mr. NATSIOS. Well, USAID administrators, Peter McPherson, who was USAID administrator under Reagan, and Brian Atwood under President Clinton and I argued in a an article we wrote for Foreign Affairs in late 2008 that the U.S. Government should go back to the model for managing aid under President Nixon when he became President. He recentralized all of the aid programs in one place, USAID.

If you wanted to get other domestic agencies involved—for example the U.S. Geological Survey has seismologists. I mean, USAID does not have seismologists, so USAID would sign interagency agreements to bring their expertise into development programs on disaster preparedness. These domestic agencies had to report to AID and perform or they would be shut off from money.

That is not the case now. We have two dozen different agencies in the Federal government doing aid programs all over the world, and they do not report to anyone frankly.

Senator PERDUE. I understand.

Mr. NATSIOS. And they do not report to you, I might add. These are domestic—they report to domestic committees, and oversight committees domestically do not know anything about this. It is the Foreign Affairs committees that should have the oversight, not all these domestic oversight committees of the Congress in my view. So I have advocated with my colleagues—with Brian Atwood and Peter McPherson in an article that came out in Foreign Affairs in October/November of 2008 to restructure the whole system very substantially to put these functions back in USAID the way—and Nixon did this, and I might add, with support and help from Hubert Humphrey, interestingly enough. The old adversaries, they got together on these reforms in the—in the late 1960s after Nixon had defeated Humphrey for the Presidency. But on this they agreed. We needed a strong aid program.

Two, it is not quite true to say this is new. In the 1980s and the 1990s, we have the Development Fund for Africa, and it was performance based. A country had to perform to get the funding. This concept is not new. We had in place, and because of all the massive cuts in aid in the 1990s after the end of the Cold War, the whole program was shut down, and the program collapsed.

So there is—there are roots in the past, and we do know it can have an effect because we can show that from the record of the 1980s and early 1990s.

Senator PERDUE. Thank you. Thank you, Mr. Chairman.

Senator CARDIN. We are going to go into a very short recess. The chairman will back in a moment to continue. There he is. We are not going to go into recess.

The CHAIRMAN [presiding]. Thank you all. And whether there are a lot of members here or not, it is good for our record. It is much appreciated. I know you will have other questions. I ran to go vote. I know they are going to do the same. I doubt either one of them will be back. And I did not hear the question Senator Perdue, so I apologize if I end up being redundant.

The other two witnesses—Congressman Kolbe and Dr. Birdsall—is it your opinion that, in essence, the effectiveness of USAID programs, which I know is not the focus today, really has been in many ways minimized due to State's involvement in other strategic interests? Is that something that the two of you share?

Dr. BIRDSALL. I think it is actually reasonable to see some of the work of USAID as directed to countries that are strategically important at key moments for the U.S. I do not think that is the issue. I think the difference between MCC and USAID is that MCC had a fresh start. It is not encumbered with—I think you were not here when I said that USAID after 50 years is encumbered with a lot of earmarks, and directives, and informal mandates.

And, therefore, USAID as a bureaucracy has grown various forms of risk aversion, what Andrew Natsios calls the counter bureaucracy, which is the inspector general functions. All of these make sense, but after 50 years I do believe it is time to ask USAID to come back to Congress and explain what of these encumbrances might help liberate it to behave more along the lines of the MCC model in those countries that are ready with good government to maximize the impact of U.S. taxpayer support. That is the difference.

So I would not support at the moment moving the MCC, somehow sticking it inside USAID or sticking its functions inside USAID. I think that would be misguided. We have something that works. It works very well. It is adhering to the model that Congress mandated at the time of the legislation. And, you know, I would move in the direction of helping USAID undo some of the accretion of burdens that it labors under and that make it less effective.

The CHAIRMAN. Congressman Kolbe.

Mr. KOLBE. Well, I would agree that I do not think that the answer is to put the MCC into USAID. I would disagree with my good friend, Andrew, on that. He is right that there are precedents for this. There are roots that are found elsewhere. But I think the differences, as he said, there are some 30, 40, maybe as many as 50 different agencies in the U.S. government that have some of its finger into the area of foreign assistance in one way or the other. So the addition of the MCC is not as though you are really adding that much more to the—to the explosion of these agencies.

Why I think MCC is different is that it has taken the criteria, performance based as he talked about, in USAID. It has taken it and put it into writing into the law, into the standards, and I think that has made a difference. It has had—instead of changing with each country or with each kind of project you go to, there is a set of criteria to qualify before you even get to the threshold. And I think that has made a huge difference in these countries and in the kind of assistance that we have given.

And I think it has been transformational. If you were to ask me the single most important thing that I think USAID or that the MCC has been able to do has been to change the way these countries think and to try to get into the MCC to make changes internally in their own laws in their countries.

Mr. NATSIOS. Could I just add something, Senator?

The CHAIRMAN. Yes, sir.

Mr. NATSIOS. There are basically four or five different ways to allocate money through aid programs, regardless of which donor government you are in—Britain, Germany, the United States, Canada—countries that have aid programs or the World Bank. One is a performance-based system. The Development Fund for Africa that I mentioned earlier in the Reagan administration and First Bush administration were performance based. The MCC is performance based.

There are need-based programs. A third of all our aid, $10 billion, goes to health programs, about a third. It is the largest sector by far. It is a need-based program. You would not send aid to a country based on their performance for malaria programming. What if they did not have any malaria? I mean, there is no point in having a malaria program if there is no malaria in the country.

We respond to health needs, and the AID program actually has a rigorous set of indicators that it uses to allocate money unless the State Department interferes. And when I say they interfere, we should have had an HIV/AIDS program in India or Russia because they had the highest rates of increase. When I was AID administrator, the decision was made over our objections to put it in Vietnam. There was no reason to put in Vietnam except a strategic one, which is we wanted an aid program there, and we did not want anybody complaining about it in Congress.

But from a technical standpoint, it should not have been in Vietnam. It should have been India or Russia where the infection rate increases were much greater. For the most part, the HIV/AIDS program is where it should be, but there was an exception made in this particular case that was a problem.

So the third way in which we allocate is based on interest, our national interests, and that is appropriate. And AID should run those programs, but it should come out of the ESF account. Up until the 1990s, when policymakers had a strategy, like Egypt, or Jordan, or Israel, that money all came out of ESF. Now, we take it out of the Development Assistance Account. We take it, and we use the MCC for it, too.

In one case, the U.S. ambassador to the country and the USAID mission director opposed their own country getting an MCC compact because of the high level of corruption. They did not want to say it in cables because they were afraid their opposition would be leaked and it would cause a huge furor. They came back to Washington to try to stop the compact because they said the country clearly did not qualify.

The CHAIRMAN. This is within MCC?

Mr. NATSIOS. This is within MCC, yes. And I can tell you from direct experience they told me what they said, and they were ignored. I know why they did it, State did it, for counterterrorism reasons.

The CHAIRMAN. But there is an MCC board.

Mr. NATSIOS. No, the board was not—the board ignored the indicators and approved the compact. You know, the thing is I used to sit in those meetings as AID administrator. The chairman of the board is the Secretary of State. Just think of who the four secretaries of state who were under the MCC: Colin Powell, a historic figure, Condi Rice, Senator Clinton, and John Kerry. You are going to sit there and argue as a Federal official with the Secretary of State sitting there who is insisting that they ignore the indicators? I think maybe having the Secretary of State appoint someone, but not him or herself sitting as the chairman of the board, would be much wiser.

The CHAIRMAN. Do the other two witnesses agree?

Mr. KOLBE. It is an interesting concept, and in an ideal world I think that would be right. But I do not think practically speaking you could substitute for the Secretary of State. I think the Secretary of State has to be in that position.

The CHAIRMAN. And tell me why you say that.

Mr. KOLBE. Just because I think of the role that the Secretary of State plays in the overall foreign policy of the United States, and I think it is the most significant position and the most significant role. And I think it would be difficult to substitute somebody else in that position. I think politically it is difficult. I am not sure it could fly here in Congress or fly with any administration.

Mr. NATSIOS. I agree with you. I do not think it would fly politically.

Dr. BIRDSALL. There are in the world——

The CHAIRMAN. So let me just if I could, and I want to hear from you, too, Dr. Birdsall. But it seems to me that what you are saying validates some of the criticisms directed at MCC that some of the decisions that they are making are not economic, but based on other interests. And it seems to me that a great way of nullifying that would be to ensure that the Board was, in fact, truly independent. So I am a little confused by the response.

Mr. KOLBE. Well, I think maybe you were not in the room when I said that I did disagree with Ms. Hyde in that there had not been pressure on the CEO or on the MCC or to not succumb. I agree with Andrew that there have been times, and I think there have been times when it has succumbed to that pressure.

But by and large, I think it has worked. I think it has worked—in terms of what it was designed to do I think it has worked. As he has pointed out, there are other projects that are specifically designed to focus on our national security needs, and those, as he said, should be done out of ESF.

But I think the Millennium Challenge Corporation, it is not perfect, but I do think it has worked by and large as well as can be expected, and it can be improved. And as I said in my testimony, I think one of the roles of this committee and of Congress is to be sure that it does have the independence. One of the things that could be considered would be to add another outside director so that you would have five independent directors and four from government agencies. It was deliberately done the other way around. I might add when the draft came up from the Bush administration, it had zero outside directors on it. It was all government. And that was one of the things that we changed to make sure there were outside directors for it.

The CHAIRMAN. How are those outside board members selected today?

Mr. KOLBE. They are selected through a list that is provided by the Majority Leader and the Speaker of the House to the President, and he selects from that. So it is bipartisan.

The CHAIRMAN. But, in essence, the administration decides who is on the board.

Mr. KOLBE. Well, but picking from a list that is submitted by the leadership in Congress.

The CHAIRMAN. And how broad is that list typically?

Mr. KOLBE. It is pretty small, the number that is submitted.

The CHAIRMAN. So then by virtue of that, basically the two leaders are deciding.

Mr. KOLBE. Correct.

The CHAIRMAN. They submit two names each, and——

Mr. KOLBE. And the minority leaders.

The CHAIRMAN. Yes. Yes, I got it.

Mr. KOLBE. So it is the Speaker and Majority Leader in the House and Senate, and the minority leaders in both.

The CHAIRMAN. Dr. Birdsall.

Dr. BIRDSALL. There are type one errors and type two errors in the world, and we are focusing here on a type on error. I would— I would be very careful about mandating some change in the current arrangement. I would want to hear the examples that Andrew has in mind, how egregious were they.

I have a vague recollection in the early years of Georgia being one of the countries that was made eligible for MCC. It was close on all of the other—on all of the various measures, but it did not meet one or two of them. I would be interested in getting back to the committee after consulting with staff at CGD who know more about this.

I am much more concerned about type two errors. I am not sure you heard all of my testimony. There are a number of countries— I mentioned Tunisia, I mentioned Mongolia—that may not be eligible for another compact because of an increase in its GNI per capita. These are countries that can still—they would pass MCC eligibility on all other measures other than this extremely crude need-based GNI per capita where there are millions of people that are far from middle class, far from working class.

So my view is that that—that Congress should ask MCC to look more carefully at that measure because the type errors are far more important where the MCC model is cut off or never gets started in countries like Tunisia in a very difficult neighborhood, GNI per capita now over $4,000. It does not make sense to me. It takes longer to develop the institutions and make the investments that MCC can support so that a country like Tunisia is a little bit more solid and entrenched as a democracy that is working well for its people.

The CHAIRMAN. And those standards are set by Congress right now, the GNI?

Dr. BIRDSALL. The GNI is in the legislation.

The CHAIRMAN. Yes. Yes.

Mr. KOLBE. Could I just——

The CHAIRMAN. Yes, sir.

Mr. KOLBE. Could I just add something to that? She used the word "close," and I think that is an important point here. Part of the problem as I see it with the MCC is the must pass criteria of corruption, which I think is an important standard. But the data is weak on that, and the countries tend to cluster right around the medium, so it is very easy for one to go just above or just below that we think really does not qualify. It moves from one side to the other.

That is why I mentioned in my testimony that I think we need to do some work looking at ways we can strengthen the corruption index and get better data involved. I do not have the answer to that here today, Senator, but I think that is one of the things that does need to be looked at.

The CHAIRMAN. Okay.

Mr. NATSIOS. Senator, if I could, I put in my testimony an alternative to the current board structure because I completely agree with Jim that the Transparency International Corruption Index is widely used but it has problems.

But what they do is they send surveys out to the business community in the country and ask, did you have to pay a bribe to get the government to approve something? Do you know what happened in one country? It was Kenya, at the time one of the most corrupt countries in the world. All of a sudden there is a big change in their ranking. The political leaders apparently went to the business community and said, you are embarrassing us by answering the surveys that you have to pay bribes. And all of a sudden Kenya has improved in the rankings.

The same thing happened in the Philippines. Look at the Philippines' indicator. They moved from 141 out of 172 countries, one of the worst in the world. Now they are 85. There has not been an improvement in corruption problems in the Philippines. It is because they went to the business community and lobbied them to stop writing bad things in these questionnaires.

A better standard on the corruption index would be the rule of law. We can assess the rule of law, and the independence of the court system, and how corrupt the police are, and how abusive the police are in these countries. The rule of law—in fact, empirical evidence, the most important factor that causes state failure is the collapse or the nonexistence of the rule of law or very weak rule of law.

Governance is central to a state collapse, and the empirical evidence from scholars on this is overwhelming. We used to think it was, whether there were tribes and ethnic or religious groups fighting all of it is actually of peripheral importance. The centrality of the cause or the central reason for the cause of state failure is the absence of the rule of law and bad governance.

And so, that in my view should be a standard that a country, if you cannot get above, you should not be eligible. But I would not use the corruption index alone because it is a questionable methodology. So I agree with Jim entirely on that, and I did put this in my written testimony.

The CHAIRMAN. Do all of three of you—I guess one of the reasons for this hearing today is a push towards regional compacts. Just based on what I have heard, can you share with me your feelings about allowing MCC that flexibility?

Dr. BIRDSALL. I support that. I think that the Congress should give—should authorize at least one pilot project at the regional level. What I said when you were not here is that we know from the experience of the World Bank and the African Development Bank, these are tough to do.

Bureaucracies do not even want to do them because they take a long time to negotiate. They are more complex. The costs of administering, and monitoring, and supervising are higher. And countries do not necessarily want to do if it takes away from opportunities in their own country compact. So this is an issue where huge returns are possible, especially in Africa—West Africa, as Dana Hyde said. And I think MCC has the assets to do it, both U.S. credibility that has been built up and grant-based money that can be used to crowd in private money, private domestic and foreign investment, that is central to energy and infrastructure projects. So I would— I would definitely go for that.

Mr. KOLBE. Yes, I would support it. It is logical to me. If you take a West African country whose compact has to do with building the infrastructure for farm to market roads and transportation systems, those transportation systems may lead to its border, but to a port in the next country. So you really need to have the kind of— the ability to do regional.

The best example I think that was talked about earlier with Ms. Hyde is the Golden Triangle in Central America. It is impossible to think about El Salvador's economic development without thinking about Honduras and Guatemala. They simply are an entity really to go together economically, and you really have to think about them together.

Mr. NATSIOS. I endorsed the idea in my testimony as well. I think they are much more difficult to administer and to get agreement. Many of these countries do not like each other. There is a reason they do not have trade. They put up trade barriers between each other. When I was USAID administrator, the prime minister of one country said please talk to our neighbors because they are stopping our goods from going through to a port for export.

So I think they should get the authority, but it think they are going to have trouble using it practically.

The CHAIRMAN. So if I could just to try to draw a consensus out of your testimony, first of all, if I understand what all has been said, you would prefer to see USAID move in the direction and having the freedom and the flexibility that MCC has versus it moving in the other direction. That is a consensus position. All three of you support the notion of regional compacts, even though, as has been mentioned, there are many complexities.

And thirdly, I think there is agreement that we should really be looking at the qualification standards that are being looked at, whether it is national income levels or whether it is the corruption levels, that that is something that Congress really should be reviewing. And just for what it is worth, we have had real concerns recently, on a bipartisan basis and throughout almost the entire committee, if not the entire committee, on things like the TIP report and other areas where what is supposed to be objective decision making is being influenced by an inappropriate degree of political influence, for example with respect to decisions made on Malaysia, Cuba, other places relative to other kinds of things. I do not know if it is true. I think many people think possibly that was the case.

You would call them type two errors. Would put standards at a higher level than concerns about political influence? How should we, as we leave here, think about the issue of political influence over decision making because I think there is consensus on the first three.

Dr. BIRDSALL. Can I make a comment on that?

The CHAIRMAN. Yes.

Dr. BIRDSALL. I would say that Congress could ask MCC to bring back to Congress whatever changes in the measures of corruption, for example, and in the use of those measures the application in terms of standards and this use of where a country is if it is at the median. I do not particularly—median in terms of the list of countries on, say, behavior, on spending on their people.

It is not always sensible because of crowding of a group of countries around the median. Suppose they are all spending 20 percent on education and 20 percent on health. Suppose they—more or less, you know. Slight deviations from that for a country can throw it off the list. So some of this is about wonky data issues of standard errors and so on.

So my sense is that it would make sense to ask the MCC to come back to Congress with some ideas where changes are needed, not on the general notion that there should be a scorecard, not on the general notion that the focus should be on poor countries with sensible government, but on how that is implemented in terms of recent data, better data in some areas, use of statistical measures. I see problems there. I mean, one example seems to be—I may not have it exactly right, but we could get back to you on this, that Honduras when it moved from being a low-income country to a lower-middle-income country, then different standards were attached to it, and it was missing out for some period on eligibility.

Well, in the general the question is not, you know, now it is in a higher standard group. That does not make sense. If the trend is correct, as Dana Hyde said, if it is moving in the right direction on something like corruption, you know, if it is—if it is better than it was a year ago, or two years, or three years ago, it is not sensible to cut it off, which apparently it was at risk at some point.

I mean, maybe it is a bad example because Honduras had many problems, but it clarified for me the problems with the implementation of standards that make sense in principle, how are they—what are the actual measures and how should they be implemented?

The CHAIRMAN. Well, as a result of that suggestion, I will ask my staff now to ensure that is one of the QFRs we send to the director as a result of this meeting. Any other input on those two issues? Mr. KOLBE. I would just add that I think I agree with what Dr. Birdsall, except that you might want to consider adding into that some independent analysis, recommendation as to whether it is a consortium of universities doing a study or something and not relying just on the MCC to tell you what—how to rejigger the criteria for eligibility.

The CHAIRMAN. Good suggestion.

Dr. BIRDSALL. Yes, that is a good idea.

The CHAIRMAN. That is a good suggestion. Yes, sir?

Mr. NATSIOS. I agree with Congressman Kolbe's suggestion and with Dr. Birdsall. There is a book your staff might want to read.

In fact, maybe you should not read it because it will upset you. It is called Poor Numbers by Morten Jerven and it is an academic book. And it looks at a lot of the data the World Bank has collected and different U.N. agents have collected in Africa. And a lot of it frankly is made up.

The notion that we have achieved all the MDGs, a lot of it is simply manufactured stuff for these international conferences. I am sorry to say that, but there is scholarly evidence now. It is a good book, and it is a disturbing book, that we rely too much on numbers. That is why I urged in my testimony that we use qualitative rather than just quantitative measurements because the numbers can be distorted. If you saw how they were made up in some of the finance ministries, I think you would be a little shocked.

The CHAIRMAN. Well listen, we certainly appreciate the expertise, knowledge, background, insights that all of you three have provided. If you would, there will be additional questions I know, and if you could—we are going to take questions here in the committee, without objection, to you by the close of business Thursday. If you could respond fairly quickly, we would appreciate it.

If there is any additional thoughts that you have, you know, over the next few weeks that you would like to share with our staff, we would much appreciate that.

The CHAIRMAN. And, again, thank you for helping found this. Thank you for the tremendous insights that all of you have relative to foreign aid and MCC in general.

And with that, the meeting is adjourned. Thank you.

Mr. NATSIOS. Thank you.

[Whereupon, at 12:15 p.m., the hearing was adjourned.]

ADDITIONAL MATERIAL SUBMITTED FOR THE RECORD

RESPONSES TO ADDITIONAL QUESTIONS FOR THE RECORD SUBMITTED TO MS. DANA HYDE BY MEMBERS OF THE COMMITTEE

Ms. Hyde's Response to Senator Corker

Question 1. MCC's unique performance indicators evaluate a candidate country's record of ruling justly, investing in people, and establishing economic freedom. MCC economic assistance is intended to go to recipients who embrace core values of economic and political freedom.

♦ Do the current indicators adequately capture the kind of policy environment that is needed for private enterprise to thrive and grow?

Answer. Yes, to the extent possible. The indicators MCC uses are not perfect, but they are the best available given the range of countries and available data that can be gleaned. The third party indicators on the MCC Scorecard measure a country's commitment to ruling justly, preserving economic freedom, and investing in its people and they are intended to assess the degree to which the political and economic conditions in a country serve to promote broad-based sustainable economic growth and reduction of poverty.

Countries that score well on these indicators have faster growth potential, and so are better candidates for successful partnerships, and having the type of environment that is conducive to stronger private enterprise. In fact, several indicators in the Economic Freedom category look at various aspects of the environment for private enterprise directly: (1) Access to Credit (a measure of the scope and accessibility of credit); (2) Business Start-Up (time and cost to start a business); (3) Trade Policy (a country's openness to trade); and (4) Regulatory Quality (a measure of the quality of the rules-based environment). The other indicators also all give a sense of the broader environment in which the private sector has to function, such as Rule of Law, Government Effectiveness, Control of Corruption, and the range of indicators in Investing in People, which can allude to the quality of the workforce. MCC's Board will look at all of these factors, as well as supplemental information, in gauging the overall policy health of a given country, and discuss what it means for private enterprise, among other considerations. MCC is, however, always open to considering new and better indicators and are continually engaging with stakeholders on this very question.

♦ How does MCC review the effectiveness and accuracy of the performance indicators it uses?

Answer. MCC continuously reviews the indicators it uses on the scorecard and regularly consults with a range of civil society and academic stakeholders on governance indicators in order to understand what data is available and how it compares to what MCC is currently using. This is particularly important when certain indicators have not been regularly updated or when better methodologies have been identified providing better indicators for a particular policy area.

MCC has an open door policy on this and welcomes stakeholders to discuss particular datasets, which happens often. When a change is needed, MCC will update indicators accordingly, consulting externally and with its Board before making the change. For example, in FY 2016, more comprehensive and more regularly-updated data providers were identified to capture the Freedom of Information Act and Internet Filtering sub-components of the Freedom of Information indicator. These were adopted and replaced the former datasets MCC had been using for those sub-components, and involved extensive consultations with institutions like Freedom House and the Open Society Foundation. In all cases, MCC needs to make sure the data is public, regularly updated, has broad country coverage, and has a sound and comprehensive methodology.

At the same time, MCC is also cognizant of the need to not "move the goal-posts" on candidate countries which would dilute the "MCC Effect" (the positive impact of MCC's rigorous commitment to sound policies beyond the agency's direct investments, such as policy reforms incentivized by the scorecard) and cause the scorecard to lose credibility. MCC seeks always to balance continuous improvement while ensuring prudent stability in the scorecard. Fundamental changes, therefore, such as changing the passing rules, or adding in entirely new indicators are done with a long term perspective.

Transparency is a critical element to this process and all changes are highlighted in the annual Selection Criteria and Methodology Report, submitted to Congress each September.

♦ How and why have the various indicators that MCC uses changed over the years?

Answer. The scorecard has been changed significantly twice:

FY 2004–FY 2005: Original Scorecard: 16 indicators with 6 in Ruling Justly, 4 in Investing in People, and 6 in Economic Freedom:

To pass an indicator, you had to be above the median except for inflation (be less than 15%).

To pass scorecard overall, you had to (1) pass at least half in each of the three categories (i.e., 3 in Ruling Justly, 2 in Investing in People, and 3 in Economic Freedom), and (2) pass Control of Corruption (the only "hard hurdle").

There was no Democratic Rights Hard Hurdle.

FY 2006–FY 2007: Minor Change: The Credit Rating indicator was dropped in favor of Days to Start a Business.

FY 2008–FY 2011: Addition of the Natural Resource Management and Land Rights and Access indicators:

MCC added Natural Resource Management (NRM) to the Investing in People category.

We added Land Rights and Access (LRA) to Economic Freedom.

Both NRM and LRA were added due to intense Hill and stakeholder interest in having indicators which captured land and environment issues. There was a congressional requirement that an MCC country demonstrate a commitment to "the Sustainable Use of Natural Resources" which had historically been done via supplemental information because at the time there was no good indicator to capture this. Consultation with a range of NGOs eventually led to the identification and construction of the LRA and NRM indicators by 2007–08.

MCC also combined time and cost to start a business indicators in the Economic Freedom category into one "Business Startup" indicator.

As a result, scorecard now had 17 indicators with 6 in Ruling Justly, 5 in Investing in People, and 6 in Economic Freedom.

As before, to pass an indicator, you had to be above the median except for inflation (for which a passing score was less than 15 percent).

To pass the scorecard overall, you had to first pass at least half in each of the three categories (i.e., 3 in Ruling Justly, 3 in Investing in People, and 3 in Economic Freedom), and then also pass Control of Corruption (the only "hard hurdle").

There was no Democratic Rights hard hurdle.

FY 2012–FY 2016: The Current Scorecard: MCC reviewed all indicators being used to make sure we were using best-in-class. Additionally, the agency added indicators to make sure the full suite of issues that needed to be captured were being captured, and changed the "pass half in each category" requirement to "pass half overall" in order to reduce the volatility that the Investing in People category induced and also to better reflect the economic literature which reflects that that there is no one recipe for economic growth.

MCC added two new indicators to Economic Freedom to better capture the role of women in driving economic growth, as well as Entrepreneurship: Gender in the Economy, and Access to Credit.

One indicator in Ruling Justly was replaced: Voice and Accountability was replaced with Freedom of Information because of a clearer dataset, as well as added in sub-measures of internet filtering, and Freedom of Information legislation.

MCC split Natural Resource Management into two indicators: Natural Resource Protection and Child Health, to better capture two distinct issues that had previously been combined.

MCC added a second hard hurdle. In addition to the Control of Corruption hard hurdle, a country must now pass one of the two Democratic Rights indicators, either the Political Rights or the Civil Liberties indicator.

MCC also, based on consultations with Freedom House, changed the indicator from a median pass to minimum score.

To pass the scorecard overall, a country now needed to pass the Control of Corruption indicator, pass the new Democratic Rights hurdle and pass at least 10 out of the 20 indicators overall (as opposed to half in each category).

Question 2. Countries selected for MCC compacts do not have to meet the scorecard criteria every year after a compact has been signed.

♦ Does this undermine the purpose of the scorecard?

Answer. No. Even after signing a compact, MCC's Board still looks at a country's scorecard performance since all countries are expected to maintain or improve their commitment to good governance. If a country shows evidence of a clear backing away from this commitment, MCC may take, and has taken, action including suspension or termination of assistance.

♦ Please provide the criteria according to which MCC suspends or terminates a compact.

Answer. MCC has a clear policy on suspension and termination (found here: www.mcc.gov/resources/doc/policy-on-suspension-and-termination) which lays out the three reasons that may trigger why MCC might look at the range of options available:

The Country Has Engaged in Activities Contrary to the National Security Interests of the United States; or

The Country Has Failed to Adhere to Its Responsibilities Under a Compact, 609(g) Grant Agreement, Threshold Program or Related Agreement (which could include failure to implement a compact as required or fulfill another condition which MCC required); or

The Country Has Engaged in a Pattern of Actions Inconsistent with MCA Eligibility Criteria meaning that MCC has determined that the country has taken actions that result in, or could reasonably be expected to result in, a policy reversal, a decline, or a deterioration of performance, in one or more of the policy indicators used to determine eligibility, most notably the MCC policy scorecard.

In all cases to date, MCC has taken action based on the third reason: a country has engaged in a pattern of actions inconsistent with the eligibility criteria, such as a flawed election or an undemocratic change in governance. In its most extreme form, of the 32 compacts approved to date, MCC has suspended or terminated a compact partnership, in part or in full, six times.

♦ Armenia (2008) [De facto partial termination due to flawed elections]
♦ Madagascar (2009) [Terminated due to military coup]
♦ Nicaragua (2009) [Partial termination due to flawed elections]
♦ Honduras (2009) [Partial termination due to undemocratic change in gov't]
♦ Malawi (2012) [Suspended over governance concerns; reinstated later]
♦ Mali (2012) [Terminated due to military coup]

Question 3. Every MCC compact is subject to a rigorous and data-driven impact evaluation. While these evaluations show how standards of living were raised or economic growth was created after the compact was completed, they don't address the details of how a compact was implemented, including the overall performance of the host government in meeting the demands of compact implementation.

♦ How does MCC measure progress of compact implementation?

Answer. Because implementation is in the hands of our partner country, MCC has developed a number of oversight tools to ensure the proper progress is being made in every activity the compact funds. MCC opens a Resident Country Mission, for instance, generally inside our embassy, with two direct hire U.S. nationals to provide daily oversight of compact activities. These Resident Country Missions are augmented by quarterly field visits from MCC technical experts and independent engineers that allows MCC to regularly monitor all risks including completion risk and whether funding is on budget, and then take appropriate action to manage completion risks. These actions may include terminating or descoping projects and activities.

Each quarter for each country, MCC convenes a Quarterly Portfolio Review (QPR) with management and the Country Team (including the country mission, sector experts and others) to discuss compact risks and results.

When risks are elevated, appropriate response from Headquarters staff may require more frequent site visits, extended TDYs, or mobilization of other outside assistance. When the Resident Country Mission and Washington sector experts determine a problem with project implementation exists—either because of funding issues or more common completion risks due to the five year clock -- visits and oversight becomes more frequent and a possible project rescope/deobligations may occur. Because MCC must provide a 'no objection' on all procurements and the hiring on key personal, and all funds flow from the U.S. Treasury direct to the vendor/contractor after works are certified, the agency maintains significant leverage to ensure projects are properly managed.

MCC assesses how these changes affect costs, beneficiaries, and ERRs and places key tracking indicator information on its website. Additionally, after consultations with this Committee, MCC has started to issue comprehensive compact summary reports on its website. These publically available compact-wide assessments aggregate in one place the performance indicators available as well as providing greater context for project progress and changes during implementation. Post-implementation independent evaluations are also posted here as they become available, plus original ERRs as well as updated close-out ERRs, when available.

♦ How does MCC track the progress of a nation's government's commitments to threshold programs and compacts and hold it account for its role in implementation?

Answer. Every MCC compact and threshold program includes commitments by the partner country's government to ensure successful implementation. These commitments are stated in the grant agreements and range from broad policy commitments, such as enacting and implementing reforms in a sector, to specific fiduciary obligations, such as exempting MCC assistance from taxes.

MCC tracks these commitments and holds governments to account for their compliance in several ways. The most critical commitments are typically expressed as conditions to disbursement. Every quarter, the country government must certify whether it has satisfied the applicable conditions prior to that quarter's disbursement of MCC funds. If a condition is not satisfied, MCC may withhold all or part of a disbursement of the grant. MCC has exercised this right on several occasions. For example, MCC has withheld disbursement on road construction projects in compacts until the government has reformed its road maintenance regime or increased the budget for maintenance. In policy-focused threshold programs, government reform commitments are also tracked through the monitoring and evaluation plan. For instance, the M&E plan will track whether a country is increasing its tax to GDP ratio, or decreasing commercial losses in the provision of water and electricity. MCC regularly conducts portfolio reviews of programs in implementation to track and assess progress. If a government is not meeting its commitments, MCC will engage with the government through MCC's Resident Country Mission in coordination with the U.S. embassy to encourage compliance. In extreme cases, MCC may suspend or terminate all or part of a compact or threshold program in accordance with its suspension and termination policy.

After consultations with SFRC, MCC has begun 'after-action compact reports' posted on our website that list the compacts' initial goals, economic estimates and the required conditions precedent agreed to by the countries, and then the status of those commitments and which were met.

Question 4. There appears to be a growing trend whereby certain countries have been cracking down on international NGO's and civil society through politically motivated investigations or registration laws. These actions appear designed to chill the activities of these civil society groups or drive them out altogether. It would be inappropriate to provide a compact to a candidate country that is unduly persecuting civil society.

♦ Please describe how MCC includes a government's enabling environment for civil society in its scorecard indicators?

Answer. MCC has a scorecard indicator provided annually by Freedom House, the Civil Liberties indicator, which explicitly captures this issue. This indicator measures (on a scale of 0 to 60) Freedom of Expression and Belief, Associational and Organizational Rights, Rule of Law, and Personal Autonomy and Individual Rights. Freedom House provides a full public narrative on why it scores a country a certain way on each of these issues, which allows MCC to see the trajectory over time more clearly as well as the reasons behind that trend, and to engage directly with countries on specific areas of concern. The enabling environment for civil societies cuts across all aspects of this indicator, but especially the sub-section on associational and organizational rights.

MCC's Freedom of Information indicator also captures some aspects of the enabling environment for civil society, since it includes explicit measures of freedom of the press, internet freedom and access to information. This indicators helps ensure we have a full picture, together with Civil Liberties, of what the civil society space looks like in a given country.

♦ How does MCC apprise the Board of candidate country performance on engagement with civil society?

Answer. MCC staff, including the CEO and the in-country teams, meet regularly with local civil society organizations and constantly monitor this issue in partner countries, then apprises the Board of Directors of candidate country performance regarding engagement with civil society in three ways:

1. By actively discussing the performance of the country on the Civil Liberties and Freedom of Information indicators, including their trajectory over time, and what the accompanying narratives say about the performance;

2. By actively bringing supplemental information to the Board to help show real-time developments in a country's civil society environment that may not be covered by the indicator due to data lags or issues not captured directly by the indicator;

3. By the Board members themselves—MCC's private sector members are often leading members of civil society, and will often host their own consultations with in-country civil society groups to get a richer picture of the civil society environment in a country, and brief the rest of the Board accordingly.

Question 5. MCC has a number of governance and other performance indicators to measure a country's policy performance. MCC's selectivity with respect to candidate countries was, in part, intended to lead to incentivize countries towards policy improvements. However, the compact candidate pool is faces limitations, particularly with regards to the number of eligible countries.

♦ Why does the promise of an MCC compact not act as more of an incentive for more countries to make policy changes to qualify for a compact?

Answer. MCC's high standards for governance, most readily exemplified by the scorecard which sets a clear and transparent criteria for countries to gain MCC compact eligibility, establish a high bar for inclusion in the program. There is clear evidence, dubbed the "MCC Effect," of countries working to improve their performance on MCC's scorecard in hopes of not only eventual selection for MCC compact or threshold eligibility, but also because they recognize the scorecard can provide a "road-map" for a broader policy reform agenda. From Cote d'Ivoire to Togo, Niger to Guatemala, and many more, MCC has a wide range of examples of countries using their scorecard to improve their overall policy performance. MCC meets almost weekly with country stakeholders trying to understand the scorecard, what they need to do to improve performance, and how MCC can better-connect them to the indicator institutions.

Furthermore, in a 2013 study by the College of William and Mary, when asked to identify the three most influential external assessments of government performance from a list of 18 options, respondents to an independent survey of development stakeholders repeatedly identified MCC's scorecard eligibility criteria.

In some cases, a country's pathway to change is long and the incentive effect takes time to manifest itself; that is why we see some emerging MCC partners in our second decade with whom we could not work in our first. We have found that in the presence of a government with a sincere commitment to the wellbeing of its citizens, the MCC Effect is alive and well.

Ultimately, however, there are many factors that influence a country's willingness and ability to change, and sometimes even the incentive provided by a potentially sizeable grant cannot overcome countervailing forces.

Question 6. A significant portion of MCC's funding has gone to infrastructure development. For example, over half of the MCC funding since 2004 has gone to the transport sector, mostly roads, water supply and sanitation, and energy infrastructure. Once this infrastructure is built, it must be maintained.

♦ What steps does the MCC take through its compacts to ensure that this infrastructure is adequately maintained after the MCC compact concludes?

Answer. One of our core principles is country ownership, which is the idea that countries are full partners in designing and implementing compacts. This is an industry best-practice approach that helps to ensure long-term sustainability of our investments. The ownership a country exhibits when they are developing the proposals and managing the projects helps insure sustainability. The MCA, which is the accountable entity set up by the government with a mixed government/private sector/civil society board structure, is essentially a joint venture between our country partner and the United States that ensures U.S. funded projects are implemented effectively in tight timelines without waste fraud or abuse, while fully investing the partner country government in ensuring the sustainability of our joint work.

In addition, because the agency measures the benefit streams of its investments over 20 years, MCC takes the long view with all of its projects. Each compact has conditions precedent (CPs) that must be satisfied before entering into force and, thereafter, for compact funding disbursements. MCC has begun listing these CPs on our website and tracking their success at closure. For instance, CPs on a road construction project typically will include reform to the country road maintenance systems generally, not just targeted to the MCC-funded road segments. This both enhances sustainability environment for the newly-constructed road and avoids any risk that the compact project would get special attention from government funds while other roads languish in need of maintenance. MCC also works with partner countries to establish maintenance plans once projects are completed.

For example, in Burkina Faso, MCC funds was used to put in place critical policy reforms to ensure long term sustainability of road infrastructure. In addition, MCC funded technical assistance activities that are aimed at building the institutional capacity of the road agency to develop a 5-year road maintenance plan and implementation mechanisms. MCC funds were also used to setup innovative matching funding schemes that incentivized the government of Burkina Faso to contribute long-term sustainable financing for road maintenance. Another example is Liberia where we are funding the establishment of a training center and training the technicians in the electricity sector to better operate and maintain the assets of Liberia's electricity utility that includes the Mt. Coffee Hydropower Project whose rehabilitation we are also funding.

In Jordan, where MCC funded a program to provide additional water to one of the largest cities—Zarqa—through wastewater treatment, the compact implemented several measures to instill operational and financial sustainability, including realigning and raising water and sewerage tariffs to reflect the cost of service, mobilizing private sector finance and technology to construct and operate wastewater treatment, mobilizing private company to manage and maintain all water and wastewater assets and operations in Zarqa under a performance-based management contract, and funding capital equipment and training for the maintenance of sewer trunk lines.

Progress on these promises by the government are tracked and will factor into possible considerations of a subsequent compact.

Question 7. MCC is currently limited by law to using no more than 25% of its budget for lower middle income countries. Some argue that the pool of lower income countries is shrinking as Lowering Income Countries (LICs) graduate up to Lower Middle Income Country (LMIC) status.

♦ How do these limitations impact MCC's work?

Answer. The current definition of candidate countries as only low and lower middle income countries may not capture "need" adequately. Substantial poverty exists outside of low income countries, and increasingly, donors are adjusting their operations to reflect this view of the world. MCC is exploring whether other measures of poverty and well-being exist—ones that may better capture countries currently excluded but that are, by most reasonable estimates, still very poor. For example— looking at median income levels, different poverty indices, or inequality measures. Because MCC's overall appropriations level is significantly smaller than originally envisioned, the 25 percent cap for LMICs means the agency is limited-even more so than originally intended-in its ability to support and spur sound economic and social policies and good governance in countries that may have widespread and per- sistent poverty and to work with them to promote poverty reduction through economic growth.

Ms. Hyde's Response to Senator Cardin

Question 1. In his written testimony, Mr. Natsios suggested that given the limitations of the underlying data behind the control of corruption indicator, the hard hurdle for candidate countries should be replaced with the rule of law indicator.

a. How does the data quality between these two indicators compare?

Answer. The underlying quality of the data for the two indicators is essentially the same, with 19 of the 21 sub-sources comprising "Control of Corruption" and "Rule of Law" coming from the same source, although the specific survey questions asked and other data pulled from those sub-sources are different for each indicator. Both the "Control of Corruption" and "Rule of Law" indicators are produced annu- ally by the World Bank's Worldwide Governance Indicators group (WGI), and are each comprised of 21 sub-sources that are a mix of perceptions-based surveys, expe- riential surveys, expert assessments, donor assessments, and private sector assess- ments. They are produced by a range of public and private institutions such as the Economist Intelligence Unit, the Gallup World Poll, Freedom House, Global Integ- rity Indicators, among others. The Rule of Law indicator uses two sub-sources that Control of Corruption does not (Heritage Foundation Index of Economic Freedom and State Department Trafficking in People Report) and Control of Corruption uses two sub-sources that Rule of Law does not (Transparency International Global Cor- ruption Barometer Survey and Political Economic Risk Consultancy Corruption in Asia Survey).

Because the WGI group chooses specific aspects or questions from these sub- sources relevant to the concept they are trying to measure, it aggregates them using a sophisticated weighting methodology. Further details can be found here:

http://info.worldbank.org/governance/wgi/index.aspx#doc-methodology.

From the Economist Intelligence Unit, for instance, WGI will pull questions related to violent and organized crime, fairness of judicial process, enforceability of contracts, speediness of judicial process, confiscation and expropriation of property and intellectual property rights for the Rule of Law indicator, and for Control of Corruption they will pull surveys on corruption among public officials. In another example, the Gallup World Poll survey that WGI uses for Rule of Law asks, "Have you had money property stolen from you or another household member?" and for Control of Corruption asks "Is corruption in government widespread?" World Economic Forum Global Competitiveness Report's questions on the cost of crime and violence and judicial independence will go into the Rule of Law indicator whereas their questions on the prevalence of bribes in the judiciary and public trust of politicians find their way into the Control of Corruption indicator.

b. How quickly does each indicator respond to policy reforms or other on- the-ground changes?

Answer. In general, there is a one to two year data lag for both indicators. Both Control of Corruption and Rule of Law data appearing on MCC's FY 2016 scorecard, released in November 2015, are generally capturing the state of those surveyed in calendar year 2014 and the early part of 2015. Each of the institutions creating the

21 sub-sources used for the respective indicators typically updates their data on a one to three year data cycle.

> c. Is simply swapping one indicator for another in this sense the best way to incentivize potential candidate countries to tackle corruption?

Answer. Because there is no difference in data quality or time lag, it would make no difference in terms of the volatility of either indicator. The difference, though, is what type of information is more desirable to be made a hard hurdle. Control of Corruption seeks to capture the extent to which public power is exercised for private gain (including both petty and grand forms of corruption, as well as capture of the state by elites and private interests) whereas Rule of Law seeks to captures the extent to which agents have confidence in and abide by the rules of society (in particular the quality of contract enforcement, property rights, the police, and the courts, as well as the likelihood of crime and violence).

As a result, Control of Corruption is directly capturing all aspects of corruption, while Rule of Law is looking at the overall institutional strength of the country, which includes (indirectly) the ability for corruption to flourish or not flourish.

> d. Do you feel making this statutory change would preserve the intent of provision while simultaneously allowing MCC sufficient flexibility to balance the indicator score with the sometimes conflicting realities that are observed on the ground?

Answer. There is no statutory change needed. MCC's Board of Directors has the authority to change or update as needed the criteria used to determine eligibility through the annually updated Selection Criteria and Methodology Report. The scorecard is the first and primary piece of evidence the Board uses to select countries as eligible for assistance. It takes the "hard hurdles" very seriously. However, the Board uses sound judgement to analyze what the scorecards do, and sometimes do not say. It considers supplemental information on a potential partner country's economic context, investment climate, and capacity. And it must look at the overall policy performance in a country, the opportunity to reduce poverty through economic growth, and the availability of MCC funds. While swapping out one hard hurdle for another would imply switching priorities from a specific focus on corruption to a broader focus on the overall strength of a country's rules-based institutional environment, it would not necessarily change the Board's overall discretion in making selection decisions.

> e. What implications would this switch have for candidate countries? How would the existing pool of candidates fare if the rule of law indicator was made a hard hurdle in place of the Control of Corruption indicator? Are there previous compact countries that would have been made ineligible if this change had been adopted?

Answer. Because of the substantial overlap between Rule of Law and Control of Corruption, the impact of making Rule of Law the hard hurdle in place of Control of Corruption would be small. While passing the scorecard is not the only determinant of country partner eligibility, the existence of any hard hurdles, and the importance the Board places on passing the hard hurdles is, in and of itself, a limiting factor in country selection. This would be true regardless of which indicators are designated as hard hurdles.

If Rule of Law had been the hard hurdle, there were at least five countries that passed Control of Corruption when they were selected but not Rule of Law, primarily in Latin America (Honduras in FY 2004, El Salvador in FY 2006, Colombia in FY 2009, El Salvador for a second compact in FY 2012, and Liberia in FY 2013). During their compact development phase, Honduras, El Salvador, and Liberia all failed Rule of Law which would have most likely precluded signing a compact.

If Rule of Law and not Control of Corruption were the hard hurdle in FY 2016's selection round, the low income countries of Bangladesh, Kenya, and Nicaragua all would have passed their scorecards instead of failing and therefore would have potentially been competitive for selection. For lower middle income countries, Kosovo passed Control of Corruption this year but failed Rule of Law (and was selected as eligible) but Moldova failed Control of Corruption and passed Rule of Law and was not chosen.

> f. Have you identified alternative measures of corruption that could be adopted in place of the current metric, for example, Transparency International's Corruptions Perception Index? If so, what are the advantages and disadvantages of each?

Answer. Yes, MCC has spent—and continues to spend—significant effort looking at alternative measures of corruption. To date, WGI's indicator that measures control of corruption, while not perfect, is currently the best indicator available because of its scope of countries covered, how often it is updated, the transparent, evidence-based methodology and the general level of comprehensiveness in their assessments. The other alternatives miss one or more of these important conditions. For example, Transparency International's respected Corruption Perceptions Index (CPI) is not as comprehensive because it asks those surveyed how corrupt they perceive their public institutions to be, but does not dig down further and therefore yields little in terms of evidence and actionability. On the other side of the spectrum is Global Integrity's Country Reports, which rate a wide range of specific anti-corruption institutions and mechanisms in a given country and therefore ensure a wide range of evidence behind scores as well as highly specific sets of actions a country could take—such as to strengthen certain institutions or pass certain laws—however it does not satisfy MCC's need for wide country coverage and regular updates.

g. Would a hybrid of the Control of Corruption indicator and the Rule of Law indicator be practical and more informative for MCC's country selection?

Answer. Because there is such a great deal of overlap between the two indicators, a hybrid of the two indicators would not cause a big change in who passes or fails their scorecard overall. On average, 80-85% of all candidate countries either passed both indicators or failed both indicators.

As discussed above, only 5 countries would have newly passed the scorecard in FY 2016 if Rule of Law was the hard hurdle (Bangladesh, Indonesia, Kenya, Moldova, Nicaragua) while 4 would have failed (El Salvador, Kosovo, Liberia, Mozambique).

h. Would you recommend any statutory changes to allow more flexibility in the application of the Control of Corruption indicator?

Answer. No. The MCC statute provides the flexibility needed. Section 607(a) of the Millennium Challenge Act of 2003, as amended, stipulates that, "MCC's Board shall determine whether a candidate country is an eligible country.[and] such determination shall be based, to the maximum extent possible, upon objective and quantifiable indicators."

The mechanics of the scorecards themselves and the Control of Corruption "hard hurdle" is not a formal part of MCC's legislation. MCC submits to Congress an annual Selection Criteria and Methodology Report (SCMR) which outlines how MCC's Board will assess countries for compact eligibility against the wide range of factors outlined in section 607(b) of the Act, including the reliance to the maximum extent possible on objective and quantifiable indictors. It is therefore MCC's annual SCMR which determines and prescribes the Control of Corruption hard hurdle.

i.Would you support Mr. Natsios' suggestion to adopt the Rule of Law indicator in place of the Control of Corruption indicator?

Answer. As discussed above, there is a minimal difference between the two indicators in terms of which countries would newly pass or newly fail, and the Board looks seriously at failure of Rule of Law when making its selection decisions. Ultimately, the issue with Control of Corruption versus Rule of Law is not which should be the hard hurdle, but rather how we can find indicators that capture all the issues stakeholders are concerned about, and do so in a way that is comprehensive, evidence-based, and highly actionable.

This is why MCC is focused on supporting efforts to create stronger governance indicators, as it is doing through the Governance Data Alliance (GDA) which is a community of data producers, users, and funders committed to the effective production and use of high-quality data to advance governance reforms in countries around the world. MCC helped form the Alliance in 2014 to address the persistence of inadequate data coverage and mixed quality in assessing a range of governance dimensions in countries around the world, and the twin challenge of data producers often lacking insight into who the actual users of their data were. No single organization can solve these problems alone, and the GDA recognizes the need for collective action to strengthen the ongoing future production and use of governance data. The Alliance addresses these problems by facilitating coordination and knowledge-sharing among governance data producers, collecting and analyzing user data and behavior to better enhance the GDA's collective understanding of target governance data users' actual needs, and developing mechanisms to ensure that governance data producers are responsive to these needs.

A first product of the GDA will be the imminent launch of a publicly-available "dashboard" that consolidates all GDA members' governance data into once place so that a user can immediately see what data is and is not available for a given country or topic, and producers can see where the gaps and overlaps are to help coordinate future data production efforts.

Question 2. What is MCC's view on the suggestion made by other panelists that Congress should amend MCC's authorizing legislation to identify a different measure of poverty than the GNI per capita metric currently used? Which metric do you feel best captures poverty for MCC's purposes?

Answer. Poverty is changing in ways that are not well captured by average per capita income measures. In the world today, the largest numbers of poor people live in marginalized pockets in middle income countries. Similarly, for countries with high inequality, measuring average per capita incomes obscures important information, as it does not show the degree to which growth is shared (or not shared) by those at the bottom of the income distribution.

The current definition of candidate countries as only low and lower middle income countries using GNI, therefore, may not capture "need" adequately. Substantial poverty exists outside of low and lower middle income countries, and increasingly, donors are adjusting their operations to reflect this view of the world.

MCC is exploring and will discuss with Congress and other stakeholders whether other measures of poverty and well-being exist—ones that may better capture countries currently excluded but that are, by most reasonable estimates, still very poor. For example—looking at median income levels, different poverty indices, or inequality measures.

Question 3. The MCC legislative mandate is to lessen poverty through economic growth. In your view, are sufficient funds being provided to each country to make a significant difference in their poverty levels?

Answer. While there are a number of factors that contribute to overall economic growth in a developing country, MCC's approach is to maximize potential impact by working in partnership with country representatives to understand and unlock the binding constraints to private investment to reduce poverty. This potential impact, however, is often limited by the funds which can be effectively absorbed by partner countries in five years as well as the available of funds MCC has to deploy. In some instances we may not be able to fund high-ERR projects due largely to budgetary limitations. In FY 2015 and FY 2016, the President proposed significantly higher funding levels for MCC. The lower amounts ultimately appropriated will require us to adjust planning going forward, however, our role is to use our limited, but still significant, grant resources to help support and spur country commitments to sound economic and social policies, good governance and investments in their own tools to accelerate and sustain public and private investment in their country's future prosperity.

Question 4. Mr. Natisos suggested in his verbal testimony that in the past, several countries had been approved for compacts that did not meet the scorecard criteria. Furthermore, he asserted that compacts had been previously awarded for geopolitical reasons. Are you aware of any such instances? How does MCC's governance structure maintain impartiality when selecting compacts?

Answer. There has only been one instance of a country being selected and approved for a compact despite not passing the scorecard, and it was in the first year of MCC's existence. Georgia failed the Control of Corruption in FY04 the first year of MCC's selection process when scorecard standards were not yet regularized, and publically available supplemental information was used to augment the information found in that case. While it was still failing the following year in FY05 at the time of compact approval, Georgia later improved their scorecard performance and subsequently passed by FY07.

Note that there have been cases of previously selected countries not passing the scorecard at the time of compact approval. The Board selects a country as eligible to develop a compact in one fiscal year, but this does not guarantee a compact. Board approval of a compact happens after the program proposal has been developed, which may be two to three years after initial selection. The Board looks at scorecard performance at these milestones and more.

MCC's Board has made 47 initial compact eligibility selection decisions since FY 2004 resulting in 32 approved compacts. Six compacts did not make it to approval, and nine compacts are currently still in development.

MCC's Board has approved 32 compacts as of December 2016. Of those 32 compacts, 5 (detailed below) had failing scorecards at the time of Board approval, and this has not happened again since Indonesia's approval in September 2011. Furthermore, except for Georgia in FY05 (as mentioned above), none failed when selected for initial eligibility and in all 5 cases, the Board noted that the failures were not due to policy backsliding since initial selection. Instead, they were due to:

1. Changes MCC made to the scorecard that caused a failure due to the addition of new indicators as opposed to a decline in scores. This happened to Namibia when it was approved in July 2008.

2. Supplemental information that accounted for data lags, such as what happened to the first Georgia Compact when it was approved in August 2005.

3. The sudden graduation from low income to lower middle income categories. The LMIC category has significantly higher medians and there is a high possibility that a country will fail in their first years of transition. Congress recognized this and provided relief for any country caught in this circumstance so that each country is allowed to remain in its income category for funding purposes up to three years before transitioning, and MCC's Board often uses the same logic when weighing the impact on scorecard performance. This happened to Morocco (approved August 2007), the Philippines (approved in August 2010), and Indonesia (approved September 2011).

MCC's governance structure helps maintain impartiality in two ways:

Structurally: MCC is governed by a Board that is chaired by the Secretary of State, but includes the Secretary of the Treasury, the U.S. Trade Representative, the USAID Administrator, and four private sector members. The private sector members are often major civil society leaders (current members include senior officials from the International Republican Institute and the Open Society Foundation), and come from both sides of the political aisle. All perspectives are brought to the table and discussed frankly in the months before a board meeting at a staff level as well as at the Board meeting by principals.

Reliance on the Scorecards: MCC's legislation in section 607(a) directs the Board to make its country selection decisions by relying, to the maximum extent possible, upon transparent and independent indicators to assess countries' policy performance. In application, as per the annual Selection Criteria and Methodology Report, this means relying on the scorecards as much as possible as a pre-requisite to selection. As a result, Board decision impartiality is ensured by the close adherence to the principle of passing the scorecard and demonstrates that the mix of indicator objectivity and multi-stakeholder governance structure works. Scorecards and the Selection Criteria and Methodology Report are made public, which holds MCC accountable to all outside stakeholders for our process and our decisions. Finally, Congress, though the normal Congressional Notification process, is able to examine country partner performance at several steps on the pathway to compact approval.

Ms. Hyde's Response to Senator Isakson

Question. The Millennium Challenge Corporation builds role models throughout the developing world. That penetration of MCC compacts and projects is high on the continent of Africa. Recently, MCC signed a compact with Benin. Can you describe Benin's path to becoming a Compact Partner? How was the MCC Effect a contributing factor to this partnership? Finally, one of the keys to economic growth in Benin is the Port of Cotonou. Please describe how Benin and MCC came to the decision to work on the Port and how will the main components of the project fit within MCC's accountability framework.

Answer. Nearly 75 percent of Benin's 10 million people live on less than $2 a day. After becoming eligible to develop a compact in May 2004, the people of Benin worked with MCC to identify constraints to economic growth and—after a consultative process with the people, civil society and private sector stakeholders—signed a compact to reduce poverty in 2007. In 2011, this program ended successfully after addressing obstacles to investment and economic growth by modernizing and expanding the Port of Cotonou, often referred to as the "lungs" of Benin; promoting land security; improving access to capital for micro- and medium-sized enterprises; and creating a more efficient judicial system. The $188.5 million Access to Markets Project improved the Port of Cotonou's security, expanded its capacity, enhanced intraport traffic flow, and invested in cost-reduction measures-all of which helped create a more modern facility prepared for increased movement of goods. The volume of merchandise flowing through the port increased from 4 million metric tons in 2004 to 7 million metric tons in 2010, exceeding the port's previous capacity. MCC's investment in the Port of Cotonou continues to contribute to economic growth and trade, while exemplifying the power of private sector-led partnerships to leverage public resources. Creating a more competitive, efficient port makes Benin an anchor for regional trade and investment. The modernized port is expected to attract more than $250 million in financing from the private sector, which will increase revenues and create more jobs.

MCC's investments doubled the capacity of the port and led to infrastructure and port administration improvements that have contributed to the competitiveness of the Port of Cotonou, which has registered a doubling of container traffic in the past decade. The port was chosen as an investment because of its centrality to Benin's economy—up to one quarter of national income is dependent on the port. During the first compact MCC applied the major elements of its accountability and quality assurance framework to ensuring timely completion of works, including regular audits, use of independent engineering services, and high-level political engagement on significant policy an operational issues. An impact evaluation of MCC's investment in the port is currently underway.

Because of Benin's continued improvement on governance and the successful completion of the 2007 compact, the MCC Board of Directors selected Benin as eligible to begin a second compact in 2011. During the finalization of that compact proposal in 2014, however, Benin failed MCC's scorecard when it failed the Control of Corruption indicator. MCC's Board decided to limit the agency's engagement in the compact development process and issued a statement saying that a compact with Benin would not be signed unless this indicator score improved. This had major repercussions in Benin's political leadership, leading Benin's President to direct his government to take a number of steps, including the establishment of a national anticorruption commission, public declarations of assets by government officials, and removal of onerous roadblocks, among other actions. In FY 2015, Benin passed the Control of Corruption indicator (and improved again in 2016) and the MCC Board restored full eligibility. In advance of signing the compact in September 2015, Benin's leadership took decisive steps to improve the policy environment for the electric power sector, the focus of the second compact, including by establishing an independent regulatory authority and committing to far-reaching sector reforms concerning tariffs, utility operations, and the environment for private investment in power generation. The steps taken by the government to tackle corruption and to improve electricity sector policy can be considered an effect of the country's engagement with MCC.

The $375 million compact signed September 9, 2015, which includes an additional $28 million contribution from Benin, is designed to strengthen Benin's national utility, attract private sector investment, and fund infrastructure investments in electric generation and distribution as well as off-grid electrification for poor and unserved households. In addition to making infrastructure investments in on and off-grid power, this compact supports the sustainability of Benin's electric power sector through professional regulation, stronger utility operations and private sector participation in generation. The investment also supports Benin's newly created regulatory authority in its efforts to conduct tariff studies and develop a rate-making and licensing framework; contribute to tariff reform; put into place the policy and institutional framework required for off-grid electrification; and introduce standards for energy-efficient household practices.

Question. I am a cosponsor of S. 1605, which would authorize regional compacts for MCC. Please elaborate on how these compacts will make MCC's work more impactful.
Additionally, please explain how these compacts will operate under MCC accountability framework, which is one of the strongest components of the MCC model. How will you ensure that mission creep does not infiltrate into MCC's work?

Answer. We live in a global economy, where growth is more dependent than ever on economic integration to increase production and efficiency and the United States is missing potential impact if opportunities to strengthen regional markets around developing nations are not considered. This is particularly true in places such as Africa—where MCC is heavily invested—and in sectors such as infrastructure—where 70 percent of MCC's $10 billion portfolio has been invested.

Poor countries can grow faster, create more jobs, and attract more investment when they are part of dynamic regional markets. Enhanced regional integration can connect those countries to export opportunities and to import factors needed for their own economic activity, such as power or water. For instance, the World Bank estimates that regionally integrated infrastructure could double Sub-Saharan Africa's share of global trade.

By approaching growth opportunities from a regional perspective, MCC will be able to make high-return investments in countries that will benefit from economies of scale. Regulatory mismatches and actual physical barriers constrain countries' ability to realize the full benefits of trade with neighboring countries, effective management of common resources, or the creation of larger consumer markets. Financial or regulatory integration, transport networks that cross borders, or management of resources like energy or water all can benefit smaller or less developed economies, which are sometimes otherwise unable to reach the scale they need to be seen as consumer markets or investment destinations.

MCC has the proven operational frameworks in place to deliver economic impact through a country-driven process, and from that has gained the trust and reputation needed to address the added complexities of regional projects. The agency is able to leverage its reputation for clean procurements, economic justification for every project and country buy-in to ensure accountability. The authority in the MCORE bill, S. 1605, will allow MCC to develop regional projects while still adhering to the agency's important country-owned processes that demand accountability.

The authority in the legislation allows MCC to maintain its very focused, data driven model for country and project selection as well as local implementation and accountability because it will allow for multiple bilateral compacts to be knitted together into a regional project. The agency framework will seek to spur economic growth through a combination of policy reforms and infrastructure, justified by rigorous economic analysis.

MCC's accountability framework will, therefore, apply to any and all potential regional partners, as with the current bilateral agreements. As with traditional compacts, there will always be a possibility that a country partner will fail to meet MCC's standards on good governance and be suspended or terminated. Because of this, MCC will look to structure regional investments to be scalable to individual country partners in the event one country is suspended or terminated.

Ms. Hyde's Response to Senator Perdue

Question 1. I was a bit troubled by my visit to MCC's office in Jakarta this August. More than 50% of the $600 million (5 year) compact for Indonesia was not subject to cost-benefit analysis. I was particularly concerned about the Green Prosperity project, which makes up for $333 million of the Indonesia compact.

♦ Can you explain to me, why was a cost-benefit analysis not completed for the Green Prosperity Project or for the procurement modernization project?

Answer. MCC performs cost-benefit analyses for our projects to create Economic Rates of Return (ERRs). This assessment is done at the beginning and the end of our projects, but how early we have sufficient data to perform this analysis depends upon the project. The Green Prosperity project in our Indonesia compact is a grant facility that is structured to solicit proposals for the private sector, select the best proposals, and then finance those proposals. This is one approach that MCC uses to leverage additional outside private sector capital. Because these proposals from the firms were solicited as part of implementing the compact, ERRs for the investments were not available at the time the compact was signed.

Importantly though, ERRs were still assessed before each proposal was funded-just not as early as they are assessed for more traditional projects. The signed compact stipulated that all grants provided through the Green Prosperity grant facility would have to meet a cost benefit test and have an Economic Rate of Return (ERR) that surpassed MCC's hurdle rate before the funds were released. Because this project was structured as a grant facility around proposals to be solicited after the compact was signed, no firm ERRs could be generated before details of the proposals were known. The Green Prosperity Facility was designed, therefore, to fund proposals that would come after the compact was signed and bring private investment to locally-driven energy production, building on a separate compact activity that works to clarify land use and licensing—a prerequisite for any successful infrastructure development in Indonesia.

The economic analysis of this project began before the compact was signed. However, the Government of Indonesia originally proposed a series of renewable energy projects to MCC based on the results of a constraints analysis that showed access to electricity in remote areas was a constraint to the country's economic development. As part of MCC's due diligence during compact development, preliminary project appraisal and cost-benefit analysis were done on a sample of projects in these sectors to inform project eligibility requirements and to show there were viable projects that could meet the full economic analysis and receive funding once the grant facility was launched. At the same time, MCC included a covenant in the compact that outlined legal and regulatory reforms necessary to attract private investment in this sector.

As a result, the Green Prosperity Facility will provide co-financing only on a competitive basis, generally Public Private Partnerships, with a valid cost-benefit analysis used to determine ERRs for each. A proposal must meet MCC's threshold ERR of at least 10 percent to be eligible for funding. After a call-for-proposals, 51 were received and reviewed, leaving 23 short-listed proposals for electricity generation by small hydro, biomass, or biogas technologies that were ultimately selected for co-financing subject to successful final negotiations. The ERR was devised by comparing the economic cost of supplying electricity via the proposed technology to the economic cost of current fossil fuel based electricity supplies.

The estimated ERRs for all 23 proposals selected for partial funding were above 10 percent, ranging from approximately 12 percent to over 45 percent. Using our ERR criterion demonstrates that the overall economic cost of supplying electricity via the proposed renewable technology in each of the 23 proposals is less than the current economic cost of supply via fossil fuels.

With respect to the Procurement Modernization Project, corruption and other inefficiencies in government procurements starve government funds which should be going to their own social services. While there is a strong intuitive link between the efficiency of government procurement and a country's economic growth, it is difficult to find hard data that meets MCC's standards to determine a baseline for measuring the quality of each procurement based on the improved practices the project would deliver. Ultimately, the project is working to provide Indonesia, and the international development community, with a better understanding of how this procurement reform effort will deliver an improvement in goods and services while addressing corruption. Some spending units have already reported savings of 16 percent and higher following their engagement with the project.

♦ Do you have information on the economic rate of return for either of these projects now? Does this green energy project offer a better return on investment than say distributing diesel generators to these remote areas?

Answer. Cost Benefit Analysis (CBAs) has been or will be done for the Green Prosperity awards before they are funded. MCC will have ERRs, as well estimates of annual economic benefit and cost streams, assumptions about the number of direct beneficiaries, unit costs and benefits, etc. for all awarded GP grants.

At this point, we have estimates for all grants that have been awarded for both energy and natural resource management projects.

On-grid: Regarding energy projects specifically, the GP Facility solicited proposals for supplying electricity into the national grid in remote areas of Indonesia ("on-grid" projects). Electricity is typically in short supply in these areas and is currently supplied mainly from a combination of fossil fuel generating units operated by the national electric utility. 51 proposals were received and after careful review 23 proposals to generate electricity by small hydro, biomass, or biogas technologies were short listed and ultimately selected for co-financing (subject to successful final negotiations and validation of the preliminary economic analysis). An ERR was estimated for each short-listed project by comparing the economic cost of supplying electricity via the proposed green technology vs. the economic cost of current fossil fuel based electricity supplies. The estimated ERRs for all 23 proposals selected for partial funding were above 10 percent, ranging from approximately 12 percent to over 45 percent. This means that the overall economic cost of supplying electricity via the proposed renewable technology in each of the 23 proposals is less than the current economic cost of supply via fossil fuel. In these remote areas off Java, current electricity supply costs tend to be relatively high due to the small scale of generating units, technical inefficiencies, and high fuel and transportation costs. Because of this, renewable technologies can, under the right circumstances, supply electricity at lower economic costs in Indonesia.

Off-grid: The Facility is currently soliciting proposals to supply electricity using renewable technologies (small hydro, biomass, biogas) to remote areas of Indonesia not currently supplied by the national grid ("off-grid" projects). As described above, ERRs will be estimated for all short listed proposals, and only proposals with ERRs above 10 percent will be selected for co-financing. Alternative sources of energy (e.g. kerosene lighting or diesel motors) often cost more than electricity. Thus we anticipate receiving a number of well thought out and designed proposals with ERRs in excess of 10 percent.

♦ Without the initial CBA on half the Indonesia compact projects, does this hinder your ability to do rigorous impact evaluations?

Answer. No. Because MCC's due diligence included sector surveys and is ensuring each Green Prosperity Project has or will have a positive cost benefit analysis before funding, the lack of an initial CBA prior to the appraisal of individual projects does not affect the ability to conduct a rigorous impact evaluation. The ability to rigorously evaluate a project depends on the clarity of project design and the implementation strategy, which a CBA simply reflects rather than informs. Building a CBA into the process of individual project (as opposed to the umbrella program) approval has helped instill in our government partners the need for objective, economically-focused criteria for project selection and award of grants. For every project in this compact, MCC is working to learn lessons from implementation and offer these to the Indonesian government and other donors, as well as to ensure the sustainability of the projects after the MCC compact ends.

Question 2. I was troubled to find that according to a study by the Center for Global Development that in MCC's first ten years, about 9% of MCC's portfolio-roughly $800 million-did not demonstrate acceptable returns at the time of project approval.

♦ Can you explain to me why so many projects were approved with either a calculated economic rate of return below 10%, or in some cases, no calculation of the economic rate of return?

Answer. MCC's Economic Rate of Return (ERR) calculation is an assessment performed to estimate the anticipated effect of our work. Our rigorous analytic framework is in place for all of our projects, though the nature of the projects will determine when or how we can calculate anticipated costs and benefits.

For traditional projects, ERR projections are available well in advance. For other projects, such as those which fund proposals solicited from the private sector or from local communities, prospective ERRs cannot be calculated before MCC has received the proposals. This is a timing issue-these projects will have ERRs, but do not have them at the time of project approval, because the proposals have not yet been received.

MCC also has introduced a practice of calculating ERRs at the end of MCC's five year investment. These closeout ERRs provide an updated estimate for the returns of the investment over its lifetime. While not all projects achieve the original estimated ERRs, the closeout ERRs help us assess our project's success, and help us learn and improve future project designs. As of October 2015, MCC has calculated closeout ERRs for 58 projects, representing $2.9 billion, with an average. ERR of 16%.

When projects are approved at lower projected estimated rates of return, MCC transparently documents the mitigating economic assumptions which tend to reflect two scenarios. The first is that MCC partner countries remain poor, with very low levels of economic activity and extremely challenging growth dynamics where useful and accurate economic data is limited. This can result in both low ERRs and difficulty in producing a useful ERR.

For instance, the ERR spreadsheets for the Burkina Faso roads, mentioned in the CGD paper, can be found on our website. Burkina Faso is one of the poorest countries in the world. It is landlocked, borders the Sahara Desert and has a gross national income per capita of $670. 80 percent of Burkina's poor live in rural areas and the country faces several severe constraints to economic growth. MCC compact investments targeted very poor beneficiaries, 68 percent of whom earned less than $2 per day. These investments were made with the understanding that the Government would adopt significant institutional and policy reforms around road maintenance, agriculture, water management and land tenure intended to improve the larger investment climate, all of which were met. However, the estimated direct benefits from the project investments were projected to be less than anticipated over the 20 year compact period. This was due in part to the difficulty of gathering sufficient reliable baseline data, especially concerning potential agricultural increases in zones connected by the roads investments, during compact development. Nonetheless, the Government and MCC expects more than 1.1 million people to benefit from the investments to improve land tenure security and land management, enhance agriculture production, expand access to markets through roads, and address primary school completion rates for girls. And MCC will conduct and share post-compact ERRs and the investments will be independently evaluated to assess whether they achieved the expected results.

Another of the projects that CGD highlights, the Namibia Indigenous Natural Products, did have an ERR below the hurdle rate at the time of investment. However, based on more current estimates of costs and benefits, the updated ERR will be higher than the 10 percent hurdle rate due to a higher demand for these kinds of natural products in the world market than anticipated. While MCC does strive for the best evidence to inform our investment decisions, and looks for those with high economic rates of return and benefits for the poorest when we approve investments, the Namibia example shows the uncertainties in the analysis.

As noted above, MCC may approve a project but, because of the nature of the investment, cannot complete the ERR until later. Both Indonesia's Green Prosperity and the Philippines' community-driven small infrastructure projects are examples of this. Even though we were able to use economic analysis to determine the project framework, because both projects are based on calls for proposals, and since that call cannot happen until after the compact is approved, MCC must ensure economically valid investments are made through stipulations in the actual grants.

In all of these cases, ERRs allow us, together with our partners, to measure and prioritize the best and most effective possible interventions. MCC will continue to make investments based on the best possible evidence that they will be cost-effective. In all cases, we will continue to share with Congress and the public the pre-investment evidence, cost-benefit calculations when projects are complete, and rigorous, independent evaluations. While even the best forecasts may still fall short when they are implemented in complex and changing environments, it is critical to use and share the evidence-from investment decisions, implementation and results-so that MCC can be held accountable and provide other USG and international donors the results.

Question 3. Looking at the Indonesia example, as well as a few others, I'm concerned about how truly independent MCC is from State or presidential priorities or initiatives. Tanzania's second compact, for example, focuses on the energy sector, making it a big deliverable for the President's Power Africa Initiative. However, about 70% of the programs (worth $285 mil/5 year compact) is lacking a cost-benefit analysis. Despite this, the compact was put before MCC's board for consideration.

♦ Why did the MCC (reportedly) not conduct a CBA of Tanzania's second compact proposal prior to consideration of the MCC Board?

Answer. MCC maintains a strong commitment to evidence-based decision-making in our programs, and works to ensure our programs are cost-effective with sound program logic that will produce real impact. MCC is committed to ensuring that our proposed investment in Tanzania meets MCC's economic analysis standards and is justified by a satisfactory economic analysis prior to compact signing. At the time of consideration, MCC communicated to the government of Tanzania, as well as the Board and Congress, that while initial economic analysis justified the projects, more analysis would need to be done and that the compact with Tanzania would not be signed until that was complete. As such, the compact and its projects have been reviewed and discussed, but not yet approved, by the Board. MCC and the Government of Tanzania continue to advance design and economic analysis work on all compact projects.

It is important to note that Tanzania's interest in, and MCC's decision to support, investments in the power sector in Tanzania and other countries is driven by the Constraints to Growth Analysis conducted by economists to help guide investment decisions.

♦ If that's the case, why was there a rush to approve projects before they are better defined?

Answer. MCC and the Government of Tanzania had been developing the compact for approximately two years before the compact was presented to the Board of Directors. Over the course of the compact development process, and prior to signing a 609g funding agreement, MCC asked the Government of Tanzania to undertake politically tough reforms to increase transparency and accountability in its energy sector. Some of the toughest conditions included the appointment of a regulator in Zanzibar, payment of approximately $37 million of the national utility's arrears to the private sector, adjusting electricity tariffs for inflation, fuel costs and foreign exchange fluctuations, and publishing technology-specific models for power purchase agreements.

The government fulfilled all of these commitments with the expectation that MCC would negotiate the compact proposal and advance it for Board consideration. The MCC Board reviewed the Tanzania Compact in September 2015, but conditioned approval on two additional critical stipulations, (1) that Tanzania be determined to be an appropriate partner for MCC as evidenced in part by passing MCC's 2016 scorecard and (2) the projects to be funded under the compact meet MCC's economic analysis standards and would be justified by a satisfactory economic rate of return (ERR).

While Tanzania subsequently did pass the Control of Corruption indicator, concerning trends of policy performance have since emerged. Because of this, MCC's compact has not been provided to the Board for approval and, in November 2015, MCC sent the Government of Tanzania a letter expressing MCC's deep concerns regarding the ongoing electoral crisis in Zanzibar and the recent arrests made under cyber-crimes legislation. This letter reminded Tanzania that all country partners are expected to maintain a commitment to good governance, which includes a strict adherence to democratic principles, and protection of freedom of expression. In December, the Board deferred a vote on Tanzania's eligibility for a second compact until relevant governance concerns had been addressed.

♦ Do you believe that MCC has maintained its integrity as a truly independent agency, as originally intended?

Answer. Yes. MCC relies on a rigorous data-driven approach to country selection and project selection. Our reliance on transparent, evidence-based, and accountable decision-making roots our independence and objectivity. Our Scorecards are built on independent third-party data. We perform Constraints Analyses before designing all of our compacts, in order to determine objectively what the binding constraints-to-growth are in each of our partner countries. We rely on these analytics and data to make key decisions.

By law, MCC's CEO reports to a Board of Directors, which consists of five individuals from the government—the Secretary of State, Secretary of the Treasury, U.S. Trade Representative, USAID Administrator and MCC's Chief Executive Officer—and four highly regarded private-sector Board members appointed by the President based on congressional recommendation and Senate confirmation. Each member brings a different perspective on how to fulfill MCC's very narrow mission. The Board's reliance on the scorecards as a critical component of selection decisions ensures MCC remains independent as it pursues its mission of poverty reduction through economic growth in the best governed poor countries.

MCC does not operate in a vacuum. The agency would be remiss if it did not work in concert with other aid agencies to ensure that our assistance is not redundant or wasteful. We carefully weigh the opportunities we have to leverage other USG (or third party donor) resources in order to avoid waste and ensure an integrated effort in our partner countries.

The combination of MCC's Board and an evidence-based approach to selecting partners and making investments help ensure the agency maintains integrity and independence in its decision-making.

♦ Why is this independence a vital part of MCC as an aid agency?

Answer. MCC was established in 2004 to be a different kind of development agency. We focus on a specific group of developing countries-those that have demonstrated a commitment to good governance and sound social and economic policies.

We work alongside them to make large, long-term investments with high economic and poverty reduction returns. We are able to tailor solutions for each country based on what the evidence says are the specific barriers to growth and poverty reduction.

When creating MCC, Congress determined that independence was necessary to ensure the funds would be used for a single purpose: making investments based on transparent evidence and analysis. The independent design and approach improves MCC's accountability and helps MCC encourage and reward developing countries for good policies.

Simply put, because MCC chooses countries based on how they perform on third party indicators and not on what any U.S. government agency or administration deems important to their short term interests, countries know that making tough political reforms will be rewarded. This clear incentive structure permits MCC to promote American governance values.

This transparent framework for encouraging difficult policy reforms benefits American businesses who wish to trade with these emerging markets. Just as important, by investing in country-driven projects based in sound economic data and local priorities, rather than Washington-based priorities, MCC is able to more effectively and efficiently reduce poverty and create economic growth in a sustainable way.

Question 4. I constantly hear feedback from constituents that we have too many federal agencies. We have too much bureaucracy. And a lot of them are duplicative. I wasn't here in Congress when the MCC was created in 2004.

♦ Can you explain to me, why do we have MCC, which has an annual budget of a billion dollars, when we have USAID doing foreign assistance with a budget of $17 billion per year?

♦ What does MCC do that USAID can't?

♦ Why create another agency?

Answer. MCC and USAID are complementary tools and both play vital roles. MCC's efforts are highly focused and mission-based towards economic growth in a small group of relatively well-governed poor partner countries as measured though objective data. We are able to tailor solutions for each country based on what the evidence says are the specific barriers to private investment as the means to accelerate and sustain poverty reduction.

MCC, however, does not work in many places where the United States has important interests, such as active conflict countries or U.S. allies which do not meet the scorecard criteria. Also, MCC does not provide humanitarian and disaster response which are core strengths of USAID. Since all MCC programs have an economic growth tie and a country-led model, a health or education program at USAID and one at MCC would look very different, for instance.

MCC has specific authorities designed to support its focused mandate and model which may not work for USAID. Congress has authorized MCC to commit funding for long-term investments in a select group of countries, work in partnership with country representatives to design and implement programs to promote growth and reduce poverty, and to create incentives for policy reform. MCC's statutory guidelines require all activities be completed in 5 years and show a high, direct economic rate of return. These requirements exclude many good and necessary development activities that the U.S. may have an interest in financing.

In sum, because the U.S. has multiple objectives and needs a variety of tools to respond, our national interests are better served by having both of these agencies addressing different objectives with complementary strengths and mandates.

With its emphasis on country-led implementation, strict discipline on economic analysis, and strong focus on building conditions for private investment, MCC's unique model works best in an independent agency. This independence has produced a culture of best practices and innovation. We have seen many of principles that MCC is testing starting to be rolled into other development programs. Consolidation into an agency with a much broader set of objectives and country partners, and with different authorities, would undermine the effectiveness of the MCC model.

Question 5. As you've discussed, MCC's legislative mandate is to lessen poverty through economic growth.

♦ Do you anticipate a measurable decrease in poverty as a result of MCC compacts?

Answer. There are a number of factors that contribute to overall economic growth and poverty reduction in a developing country. MCC's approach is to maximize potential impact by working in partnership with country representatives to understand and unlock the binding constraints to private investment in order to reduce poverty. MCC holds itself to a high standard on measuring results such as poverty reduction. Rather than just measure outputs (such as the number of farmers trained) or intermediate outcomes (such as whether farmers are actually using the new techniques), MCC is striving to show not just that poverty is being reduced, but also that poverty is being reduced because of MCC's interventions. To this end, we have examples where our programs have produced measurable decreases in the poverty of our beneficiaries in the form of increased farm sales and incomes and increased household incomes. But we also have examples where our programs met or exceeded program targets but the evaluations did not find an impact on incomes. The Morocco performance evaluation showed mixed results. For instance, although farmers participating in the Olive Tree Irrigation Project expressed satisfaction with program's activities (training and irrigation) and some reported increased farm incomes, average gross farm income in the surveyed areas declined by 13 percent likely due to adverse weather conditions in crop year 2012/2013. This does not mean later years will not see an increase in incomes based on the new training and irrigation, however. Participants in the similar Date Tree Irrigation Project reported a 7 percent increase in their average gross farm income.

Because MCC has a variety of projects, what we are able to measure also varies. For example, we have some programs with clearly defined populations who will benefit from a program (such as the individual farmers mentioned above). In these cases, we are able to design evaluations to assess direct benefits from our programs on the beneficiaries. In other cases, we are investing in large-scale infrastructure, like building or rehabilitating a road. In these cases, it is much more difficult to identify individual beneficiaries, but we can measure good proxy or intermediate outcomes. In the case of roads, these results would be defined by things like reduced vehicle operating costs and, over time, changes in the price of goods that travel along the roads to markets.

♦ Are sufficient funds being provided to each country to make a difference in their poverty levels? MCC's annual budget, after all is only roughly $1 billion per year. Can you explain?

Answer. An increase in MCC funding, as requested by the President, would enhance the agency's ability to develop high-impact compacts on an expedited timetable in key regions and to share expertise with other elements of the U.S. Government. The lower amounts ultimately appropriated will require us to adjust planning going forward, however, our role is to use our limited, but still significant, grant resources to help support and spur country commitments to sound economic and social policies, good governance and investments in their own tools to accelerate and sustain public and private investment in their country's future prosperity.

Donor funding alone will never be enough to lift an entire country's population out of poverty. MCC's role is to invest a significant (but still limited) amount of funds in a way that encourages countries to pursue sound economic and social policies and strive toward good governance, while we work in partnership to unlock some of their most binding constraints to economic growth. These actions are designed to help the countries themselves attract the public and private investment required to sustain and accelerate their development progress. By creating the infrastructure and policy environment necessary for additional investment to follow MCC's investment into our partner countries, we multiply the impact of our investment many times over.

♦ To what extent have MCC projected impacts matched actual post-compact impacts and projected outputs matched actual outputs?

Answer. MCC uses projected ERRs to estimate specific quantitative post-compact impacts. MCC is generally looking to fund projects with at least a 10 percent economic rate of return (ERR) over a 20-year period. In fact, what we have seen-in a sampling of projects recently completed-is that the average ERR upon completion is actually over 16 percent.

Across MCC's closed compacts, approximately 70 percent of the performance indicators that were tracked either met or exceeded end-of-compact output targets. In Armenia, Benin, El Salvador, Mozambique, Nicaragua and Vanuatu, over 85 percent of indicators met their targets.

We also look at results from our independent evaluations, which focus on other outcomes and results that occur in the post-compact period. These results are highly project-specific and are difficult to generalize across the portfolio. Some examples include:

In Mozambique, one out of every two people lives without access to clean water. One of our rural water supply activities showed that the program cut down on the time women and girls spent collecting water and increased consumption of cleaner water, but did not reduce water-related illness. We learned that much of the water contamination came from dirty buckets and bad storage practice after water was collected.

In Mongolia, heavy use of coal stoves pollutes the air and causes health problems. Poor families also spend up to 40 percent of their income to fuel stoves. MCC's fuel subsidy reduced emissions-even more than anticipated-but didn't change fuel costs. Households said their homes were warmer at night, suggesting users may have sacrificed fuel economy for comfort.

In Honduras, MCC helped rehabilitate a main highway and upgrade and pave secondary roads. The independent evaluator calculated that the transport cost savings would results in $547 million economic returns (from a $138m project). But it also showed that better due diligence about costs-especially full engineering road cost estimates-could have helped target more profitable roads and created more benefits.

Below is a chart that lists the percentage of outputs achieved, outcomes achieved, and both. We define an output as a direct result of an activity, such as the goods and/or services produced by the activity, and an outcome as the longer-term effect that follows directly from the outputs of an activity (for example, the number of miles of roads built is an output, while reduced transportation costs due to better quality roads is an outcome). These percentages were all achieved by the end of the compact. In those some cases when the partner country continued works after compact closeout, the percentages for those projects would increase, but this is not included in order to track the effectiveness of compact funds alone.

Percentages of Outputs and/or Outcomes Achieved at Compacts' End

Compact	Outputs Achieved (90 percent and above)	Outcomes Achieved (90 percent and above)	Outputs & Outcomes Achieved (90 percent and above)
Armenia	100	75	88
Benin	85	50	61
Burkina Faso	65	33	48
Cape Verde	57	35	43
El Salvador	93	93	93
Georgia	N/A	57	57
Ghana	58	50	53
Honduras**	63	68	66
Lesotho	63	29	50
Madagascar*	71	24	34
Mali*	76	70	73
Moldova	73	69	71
Mongolia	75	47	64
Morocco	66	31	52
Mozambique	90	75	88
Namibia	75	50	65
Nicaragua**	94	72	87
Tanzania	58	46	53
Vanuatu	89	100	92
Total	71	47	60
Total excluding terminated compacts	72	48	61

*Terminated

**Partially terminated (The % achieved should not be affected. Indicators affected by the partial termination were excluded from this count.)

♦ Are projects ever suspended or terminated due to failure to meet targeted outputs or deliverables? Why or why not?

Answer. Yes. MCC investments have been suspended for both declines in country performance on MCC's governance standards as well the performance of projects and activities in implementation. Suspension or termination of a project or activity is not uncommon given MCC's careful and regular monitoring of status. This is a benefit of day-to-day oversight, formal quarterly monitoring, and, more broadly, the limitations of a strict five-year implementation period and defined project budget. MCC monitors progress on all compact projects throughout implementation and has taken action to suspend or terminate activities when appropriate, whether for failure to meet targets, for non-performance of contractors, or otherwise. Because compact funds are actually paid directly to contractors and vendors and not to the partner governments, works that are terminated can be either deobligated by MCC and used for another country or reallocated to successful projects within the existing compact framework depending on the reason for termination or the timeline and economic analysis of the existing compact.

Several examples are provided below:

♦ The Government of Morocco proposed the Enterprise Support Project to help with two of its critical economic priorities: reduce high unemployment among young graduates and encourage a more entrepreneurial culture. High levels of unemployment in Morocco stem from modest formal sector employment generation and a burgeoning labor supply. While the overall unemployment rate in Morocco hovers around 10 percent, youth unemployment in recent years has risen to approximately double that amount. The objective of the Enterprise Support Project was to improve the outcomes of two existing high-priority Government of Morocco initiatives: Moukawalati, which translates as "My Small Business," a national program intended to address high youth unemployment rates and drive Morocco's businesses to be more entrepreneurial and competitive in the face of globalization; and the National Initiative for Human Development, a multi-year initiative aimed at creating opportunities for the poor, vulnerable and socially excluded. The project was designed to be carried out in two phases, with continuation of the second phase subject to positive results from an impact evaluation of the first phase. The pilot phase was completed in March 2012; although it met its implementation targets and showed promising trends, the impact evaluation did not show statistically significant impacts and the revised economic rate of return did not justify scaling up the project for a second phase. MCC did not continue with a second phase and the project was closed in May 2012.

♦ The Mozambique Nacala Water Supply Project was terminated because the contractor failed to perform, despite the issuance of multiple cure notices and warnings from the engineer and the client, MCA-Mozambique. The contractor's inability to perform jeopardized the timeline, and we reached a point during the implementation period that keeping the contractor would prove problematic for MCA-Mozambique after the conclusion of the compact. Though the project design was sound and, if constructed, would have delivered as designed, the project was halted because of contractor performance issues.

♦ In the first Ghana Compact, the Agricultural Credit Activity was terminated when sub-loans were not being repaid. About $19.6 million was disbursed to sub-borrowers in 2009. Most of these sub-borrowers were smallholder farmers cultivating less than 2 hectares. Due to a high percentage of the portfolio at risk, MCC halted further lending in 2010 and undertook a series of measures with its Ghanaian partner, the Millennium Development Authority (MiDA) to recoup the on-lent funds. MCC requested MiDA to engage a forensic auditor to ensure that funds were not diverted. The audit concluded that there was lax oversight by the implementing entity, the Bank of Ghana. Due to this laxity, MCC issued a demand letter to the Bank of Ghana requesting that it repay $6.7 million; these funds were paid in February of 2013.

Question 6. It has been more than 4 years since the first MCC compacts ended, and so far, only a handful of evaluations have been publically released. Nineteen compacts with more than three dozen sub-projects ended more than one year ago.

♦ When do you expect we will see evaluations of these completed projects? Will you notify my staff when these evaluations are complete?

Answer. MCC's independent evaluations are generally conducted 2-4 years after our compact projects end. This is to give the projects sufficient time to ensure that benefits accrue and that expected results can be measured in a way that is meaningful. All of our program evaluations are posted on our evaluation catalogue online, and we will alert Congress, including your staff, when these are posted. In addition, MCC collects data during compact implementation, which allows us to monitor progress and make any adjustments necessary.

MCC's Monitoring and Evaluation Team is constantly working to add more evaluations to this catalogue. As of December 2015, MCC had completed and posted 14 impact evaluations (which measure our projects' impact on poverty reduction) and 27 Performance evaluations (which measure our project outputs, like number of farmers trained or miles of road paved). An additional 31 impact and 46 performance evaluations are underway or planned. These evaluations will continue to be released as the evaluators finish their analysis.

♦ Why is it taking so long to produce these evaluations?

Answer. MCC's evaluations include not only immediate outputs of the investments, but also analyze the long-term impacts of these investments. As the impact from a project may take time to be realized, MCC endeavors to collect data after enough time has passed for the effects of a project to be fully realized. Evaluations-especially impact evaluations, which measure long-term effects on poverty reduction due to MCC projects-take time. Impact evaluations are often conducted years after projects are completed. For example, the impact on farm income from training farmers on new growing techniques may not be seen for one or two growing seasons after the implementation of the new techniques.

Impact evaluations are often not finalized for several years after a compact closes, in order to better analyze the long-term impacts of our investments. They are conducted by independent firms under contract to MCC. Performance indicators are tracked quarterly and are available on MCC's website in a document called "Key Performance Indicators."

78

Question 7. MCC is taking on a lot of infrastructure programs-roads and energy infrastructure, specifically. These compacts only last five years, but most of these projects will need proper upkeep and maintenance.

♦ What steps does MCC take to ensure that its programs, especially those building infrastructure, are maintained after the MCC program concludes?

Answer. One of MCC's core principles is country ownership, which is the idea that countries are full partners in designing and implementing compacts. This is an industry best-practice approach that helps to ensure long-term sustainability of our investments. The ownership a country exhibits when developing the proposals and managing the projects helps ensure sustainability. Each compact partner establishes an "accountable entity" (known as the MCA) through which the country implements their compact program. MCAs have governing boards that include government, private sector, and civil society members. MCC's implementation oversight includes direct daily interaction with the MCA entity leadership and staff. The structure of the MCA and its close working relationship with MCC supports effective implementation on tight timelines, without waste, fraud, or abuse, while also ensuring that the partner country government is fully invested in ensuring the sustainability of our joint work.

In addition, because the agency measures the benefit streams of its investments over 20 years, MCC takes the long view with all of its projects. Each compact has conditions precedent (CPs) that must be satisfied before entering into force and, thereafter, for compact funding disbursements. MCC has begun listing these CPs on our website and tracking their success at closure. For instance, CPs on a road construction project typically will include reform to the country road maintenance systems generally, not just targeted to the MCC-funded road segments. This both enhances sustainability environment for the newly-constructed road and avoids any risk that the compact project would get special attention from government funds while other roads languish in need of maintenance. MCC also works with partner countries to establish maintenance plans once projects are completed.

For example, in Burkina Faso, MCC funds was used to put in place critical policy reforms to ensure long term sustainability of road infrastructure. In addition, MCC funded technical assistance activities that are aimed at building the institutional capacity of the road agency to develop a 5-year road maintenance plan and implementation mechanisms. MCC funds were also used to setup innovative matching funding schemes that incentivized the government of Burkina Faso to contribute long-term sustainable financing for road maintenance. Another example is Liberia where we are funding the establishment of a training center and training the technicians in the electricity sector to better operate and maintain the assets of Liberia's electricity utility that includes the Mt. Coffee Hydropower Project whose rehabilitation we are also funding.

In Jordan, where MCC funded a program to provide additional water to one of the largest cities—Zarqa—through wastewater treatment, the compact implemented several measures to instill operational and financial sustainability, including realigning and raising water and sewerage tariffs to reflect the cost of service, mobilizing private sector finance and technology to construct and operate wastewater treatment, mobilizing private company to manage and maintain all water and wastewater assets and operations in Zarqa under a performance-based management contract, and funding capital equipment and training for the maintenance of sewer trunk lines.

Progress on these promises by the government are tracked and will factor into possible considerations of a subsequent compact.

RESPONSE TO ADDITIONAL QUESTIONS FOR THE RECORD SUBMITTED TO CONGRESSMAN JIM KOLBE BY MEMBERS OF THE COMMITTEE

Congressman Kolbe's Response to Senator Corker

Question. The current Board membership of MCC consists of five public sector appointees and four private sector appointees. The MCC's mandate is to seek poverty reduction through economic growth unencumbered by important but unrelated noneconomic foreign policy objectives.

♦ Given the strong public sector representation on the Board, what would be the benefits of greater private sector representation and what should be the proper ratio?

♦ What, in your view, would be the downside of allowing the board to vote for its own chairman as opposed to having the Secretary of State have the position by statute?

Answer. I think this is a rather novel idea and one that should be explored with the administration. There will be significant pushback from State and the WH, but it is worth seeking their views on this.

Arguments in favor of this approach:

a. Would give more independence to the Board
b. Might permit an individual, such as one of the private members with more time and direct interest to serve as chair.

Arguments against this approach:

a. There will be a tendency on part of the government board members to defer to SOS as Chairman, giving them an almost insurmountable bloc of votes to elect the Secretary every time.
b. State might use this as an excuse to undermine the effectiveness of the MCC and perhaps even actively work against its annual appropriation.

Question 2. Concerns have been raised in recent years that non-economic considerations may have played a decisive role in granting some compacts in recent years.

♦ Do you share the concern that in some cases, MCC decision making may be unduly influenced by broader foreign policy or other priorities unrelated to economic development? For example, should we be concerned that a country might receive a compact based primarily on strategic considerations and not on economic development grounds?

Answer. Absolutely. This has been the case on several different occasions. Only once,, however, did the Board overtly violate the rule, that in the case of designating Georgia as eligible for an MCC Compact. That is why the charter for MCC must be very clear on this matter. The Congress must conduct periodic oversight, including examination of the minutes of Board meetings to see if these pressures are being applied. And that is why the private members of the Board are essential as they will have the purposes and objectives of the MCC more clearly in their focus than foreign policy executives from the administration who naturally have other considerations in mind for the uses of a Compact.

♦ Please describe ways to improve MCC Board governance to prevent undue influence being exerted with the intent to make Board decisions based not primarily on economic development grounds but on larger foreign policy strategic interests.

Answer:

a. Strengthen the language of the charter.
b. Periodically include report language in the appropriations bill calling this issue to the attention of the executive branch when Congress believes undue influence is being exerted.
c. Increase the number of private members of the Board of MCC

Question 3. There appears to be a growing trend whereby certain countries have been cracking down on international civil society NGO's through politically motivated investigations or registration laws. These actions appear designed to chill the activities of these civil society groups or drive them out altogether. It would be inappropriate to provide a compact to a candidate country that is unduly persecuting civil society.

♦ Should Congress consider adjusting the indicators to include an evaluation of the enabling environment for civil society in a candidate country?

Answer. This tendency might be a reason to strengthen the indicators to include this as an evaluation point. I think the indicators already touch on this, but perhaps need to be made more explicit. Certainly, persecution of civil society should be considered as important as an indicator on rule of law, transparency or commitment to education or health care.

♦ Should the MCC develop internal reporting requirements so that the MCC Board, before approving a country compact, is fully informed and in a position to evaluate whether the candidate country has been taking actions intended to discriminate and discourage civil society groups from engaging in legitimate democratic development?

Answer. It should be part of the normal evaluation process and included in any report to the Board which proposes to designate a country as compact-eligible. I don't think these should be separate reporting requirements, but should be included in the usual process of approving a country for a compact.

Congressman Kolbe's Response to Senator Cardin

Question 1. What are your recommendations for reforming the control of corruption indicator? In your view, what is the best way to measure and hold countries accountable for tackling corruption while simultaneously providing MCC the flexibility to interpret data in the context of on-the-ground realities?

Answer. There needs to be an objective measurement for corruption. Unfortunately, the current indicator is flawed in that it relies on a survey of companies doing business in the country. More emphasis needs to be put on rule of law, which is a more certain way of tackling corruption where it exists.

Question 2. With the rise of more middle income countries in the developing world, the world's poor will be increasingly located in countries outside MCC's current focus. Is the current approach to measuring poverty adequate? How might the MCC respond to this changing face of global poverty?

Answer. The MCC measurement needs to be adjusted so that it can have broader authority to make compacts with countries that might have been considered the "poorest of the poor" when the MCC was created, have now advanced to low income countries. This is a positive development for the world and people in poverty, but MCC should be adjusting its sights to adapt to the changing conditions. If our objective is to continue raising the standard of living for the world population, then MCC must adjust as the rising tide lifts country incomes upward.

Question 3. The MCC legislative mandate is to lessen poverty through economic growth. In your view, are sufficient funds being provided to each country to make a significant difference in their poverty levels?

Answer. The original plan for MCC was to gradually increase its appropriation for compacts to $5 billion. We have never come close to achieving this and, indeed, have found funding levels frozen at approximately $1 billion for several years. This prevents MCC from entering into compact that might have deeper economic impact.

Congressman Kolbe's Response to Senator Perdue

Question 1. Here we are about 10 years post enactment of MCC. In your view, is MCC living up to your original intent for the enacting legislation-specifically with regard to true independence from other foreign policy objectives?

Answer. Yes, I think it has lived up to its potential, which doesn't mean it couldn't do more or do better. In contrast to a lot of agencies created by Congress, this one has stuck to its mission and within the parameters of limited funding has fulfilled its objectives. There have been constant attempts to chip away at its independence by substituting criteria other than economic development for poor countries showing promise with better than average governance standards. But for the most part, the Board, largely as a result of the independence it gains from outside, private sector directors, has hewed to its mission.

Question 2. I look to projects like Indonesia and Tanzania, which were presented to the MCC Board without the requisite cost-benefit analysis, and in my view, seem that they match up a little too conveniently with other presidential or administration initiatives and objectives. Is MCC maintaining its integrity, as you intended at the time of drafting this legislation?

Answer. Not being involved in day to day MCC operations, I don't feel qualified to comment on this question except to say generally, as stated in the response to the question above, that I think MCC had adhered by and large to its original objectives. Congress and the Board needs to be constantly attuned to this issue and conduct proper, rigorous and frequent oversight to be sure the objectives are being met.

Question. I certainly appreciate the mission of MCC—reducing poverty through economic growth. However, I constantly hear feedback from constituents that we have too many federal agencies. We have too much bureaucracy. And a lot of them are duplicative. I'm sure you heard similar things from your constituents when you were in Congress. I wasn't here in Congress when the MCC was created in 2004.

♦ Can you explain to me the debate surrounding MCC at the time of its creation?

Answer. The debate at the time of creation centered around the question: could we deliver aid in a fundamentally different way, one that made the recipient country responsible to developing a plan, for meeting the criteria for eligibility and avoided most of the bureaucratic conditions put on other American assistance such as "Buy America?"

♦ Why do we have MCC, which has an annual budget of a billion dollars, when we have USAID doing foreign assistance with a budget of $17 billion per year?

Answer. USAID has a very different mission. Its assistance is given for a variety of purposes, most of which are pout into law by Congress, and does not singularly look at how assistance might be done if truly in a partnership with the recipient country, freed of bureaucratic restrictions, and based first and foremost on achieving standards of governance that have never been a part of USAID's requirements.

♦ What does MCC do that USAID can't?

Answer. See answer above. Its objectives and criteria for qualification for aid are fundamentally different from USAID. Both have a mission and purpose. USAID has a multiplicity of goals with its assistance, from improving health or education, to promoting democracy and human rights, to promoting gender equality and to some degree economic development. MCC is singularly focused on the latter.

♦ Why create another agency?

Answer. Because it would have been impossible to achieve the same goals established in law for MCC within the existing structure and culture of USAID.

RESPONSE TO ADDITIONAL QUESTIONS FOR THE RECORD SUBMITTED TO ANDREW NATSIOS BY MEMBERS OF THE COMMITTEE

Mr. Natsios's Response to Senator Corker

Question 1. For many years after its creation, MCC was criticized for its slow disbursement rates. Many, including you, have said that a large part of the reason for the problem has been weak institutions in recipient countries.

♦ In your view, has this problem been solved? If so, what lessons can we take away from these experiences with weak recipient country institutions?

Answer. What distinguishes highly developed from underdeveloped or poor countries is the legitimacy, density, productivity, and resilience of indigenous institutions-governmental, private sector, and non-profit. USAID in its earlier history used country institutions to spend aid dollars and programs suffered from low disbursement rates (and accountability problems) which Congress, the IG and the GAO objected to. USAID moved in the 1990's to NGOs and development contractors to implement programs which increased the disbursement rate and reduced bad audit findings. Development is all about trying to build local institutions. If Congress wants USAID or the MCC to move money through local institutions, disbursement rates and accountability will suffer.

Question 2. MCC supporters have long pointed to the "MCC effect" as an important component of its value as a foreign aid program. These supporters claim that the good governance indicators incentivize and encourage policy reforms in candidate countries. Clearly, countries that receive compacts have been rewarded for their good governance efforts.

♦ To what extent has the promise of a compact actually led to countries taking meaningful steps to change their policies to meet MCC standards? Has the promise of a compact actually incentivized change?

Answer. Anecdotally (from my own experience when I served as USAID administrator) MCC standards do encourage policy reform and change. The one scholarly study done of this I mentioned in my testimony suggested otherwise. I think the study was flawed as it asked hundreds of officials in each developing country whether the MCC standards affected their decision making processes and the answer in many cases was no. Reform does not begin and end with hundreds of such officials, it begins with a few very senior leaders. They are the ones who would be incentivized. To my knowledge there haven't been any studies of this small number of leaders, so we do not have academic evidence that the MCC affect works or does not work. It's an open question from an academic perspective.

Question 3. Threshold programs were originally intended to assist a country in meeting scorecard criteria. They have since been redesigned and now focus on policy reforms.

♦ Are threshold programs enough of an incentive for countries to strive for compact eligibility?

Answer. In and of themselves these threshold programs are not big enough to be an incentive, but the promise of a large MCC compact later is a large incentive that does encourage reform.

♦ Considering the modest budget request made by the President in his FY2016 budget for threshold programs (2.5%), are they even needed? What are threshold programs doing that traditional USAID programming cannot?

Answer. Traditional USAID programming can do (and have done since the inception of U.S. aid programs) all of the things that the MCC does. In fact in many ways MCC is what USAID used to be 30–50 years ago when the programs did far more infrastructure projects than they do now and were run through host country countries through government ministries. Congress has been reluctant and even hostile to giving money to USAID to do infrastructure programs except in Iraq and Afghanistan (the one place they are most difficult to do because they are a big bullseye for the insurgencies to shoot at). This is because of opposition from NGOs (which usually do not do large infrastructure projects) and from environmental groups (which fear roads, bridges, and dams open up natural habits for development).

Too much USAID money comparatively is spent on human services and not enough on good governance and economic growth. There is an imbalance in the aid system because of earmarking by OMB and by Congress to politically popular programs and an underfunding of those which are not (as they are too esoteric). USAID does not get that much money from OMB, (any) White House, or the Congress anymore to do much policy reform (with some exceptions). Money spent strategically on policy reform can (but not necessarily will) have a profound impact, but it is not easily measured in the short term nor is it easy to see how it helps poor people directly over the short term (though over the long term it they do) and thus is not particularly popular in Washington.

Question 4. Are there any adjustments to the indicators that you would recommend?

Answer. The more MCC, White House, or Congress increases the number of indicators the less affect each will have as poor countries do not have the institutional or organizational capacity to make that many changes to satisfy the demand for reform from donor governments. Few is better. As I indicated in my testimony the corruption indicator based on empirical evidence needs to be changed since it is the most important indicator statutorily. However I don't know many Senators and Congressmen who are going to vote to abolish the corruption indicator even if it is imprecise. The rule of law is a much better indicator, so perhaps the Committee could consider combining a rule of law indicator with the existing corruption indictor. That would help.

Question 5. MCC's unique performance indicators evaluate a candidate country's record of ruling justly, investing in people, and establishing economic freedom. MCC economic assistance is intended to go to recipients who embrace core values of economic and political freedom.

♦ Do the current indicators adequately capture the kind of policy environment that is needed for private enterprise to thrive and grow?

Answer. The World Bank Doing Business Report (which was almost abolished a few years ago by the WB because of pressure by countries that do not do well in the DBR index) is one of the best index on economic growth and business investment environment since nearly all of the sub-indicators which it is composed of are based on empirical evidence. I think the DBR may be used by inference in the MCC, but not directly (though I am not sure of this). USAID is the strongest supporter of the DBR in the donor community and has had a program to implement business climate reforms which we started when I was USAID administrator and continue to this day.

Question 6. There is a growing trend whereby certain countries have been cracking down on international civil society NGO's through politically motivated investigations or registration laws. These actions appear designed to chill the activities of these civil society groups or drive them out altogether. It would be inappropriate to provide a compact to a candidate country that is unduly persecuting civil society.

♦ Should Congress consider adjusting the indicators to include an evaluation of the enabling environment for civil society in a candidate country?

Answer. Increasing the complexity of MCC evaluations and indicators is not a good idea. It will simply increase the amount of paperwork and bureaucracy which costs money.

♦ Should the MCC develop internal reporting requirements so that the MCC Board, before approving a country compact, is fully informed and in a position to evaluate whether the candidate country has been taking actions intended to discriminate and discourage civil society groups from engaging in legitimate democratic development?

Answer. I would not increase the number of indicators any further for reasons stated earlier, though I am sympathetic to the argument. What would be a better idea is finding a new Governing Justly indicator to substitute for the current one which includes the environment for civil society.

Mr. Natsios's Response to Senator Perdue

Question 1. Mr. Natsios, in your testimony you criticize the decision-making process for U.S. foreign aid as being too centralized in the State Department. As the chairman of the SFRC subcommittee that oversees foreign aid, I'm interested at looking at how we do foreign aid broadly.

♦ Can you detail for me further the problems you see broadly with how we do foreign aid?

Answer. Attached to this email is an essay I wrote five years ago called "The Clash of the Counter-bureaucracy and Development" published by the Center for Global Development and an article for Foreign Affairs magazine published in November 2008 called two other USAID Administrators (Peter MacPherson under President Reagan and Brian Atwood under President Clinton) and I wrote on aid reform called "Arrested Development." These two papers describe both the problems and some solutions and though they are dated are still valid as most of the reforms have not taken place.

♦ What recommendations do you have for how we can do this better?

Answer. To summarize the two articles our foreign aid program should be reorganized structurally within the federal system, authority decentralized to the field missions, more money spent training the large cohort of new young officers who make up the USAID career staff, federal regulatory oversight over USAID and the MCC is burdensome and dysfunctional, earmarked sectoral accounts should be made more flexible, the Foreign Assistance Act simplified and rewritten, and the biggest challenge to aid programs is the (absurdly) short time horizon for outcomes demanded by Washington and the instability of funding for long term commitments.

♦ How does MCC fit into this picture? Does MCC get aid right?

Answer. It gets right some things and does not deal with other issues of central importance. The MCC has many admirable qualities the most important of which is letting countries decide how to spend aid money which they usually decide to spend on infrastructure (wisely in my view) and thus avoids sector earmarks. The MCC rewards to good performers which by definition does not include fragile and failed states (of which there are about 50 countries) which are the greatest threat to the national interests of the United States? How do we deal with these issues? MCC is one of many different approaches to aid, but what we do know is that there is no magic bullet, no optimum answer to what ails the aid system. All aid programs involve programmatic and managerial tradeoffs: aid officers must decide what the priority objectives are in order to choose one tradeoff versus another.

♦ If so, how can the U.S. foreign policy-making apparatus incorporate these lessons into other types of U.S. foreign aid?

Question 2. Mr. Natsios, you highlight in your written testimony that MCC compacts provide alternatives to Chinese loans and infrastructure development which do not encourage good governance or improved local capacity.

♦ Can you discuss in further detail how MCC serves as a counterweight to Chinese influence in developing countries?

Answer. Most leaders in the developing world know that what the Chinese offers them in aid projects has a considerable downside; the construction quality of Chinese aid infrastructure projects sometimes leaves a lot to be desired, the Chinese use imported Chinese laborers to do the work instead of local workers (which the local communities resent), the Chinese do not do much in the way of institution or capacity building (though that may be changing), and the Chinese aid programs are almost all concessional loans (subpar interest rates) which they must paid back (the USG phased out aid loans in 1982) at some point.

♦ With an annual budget of roughly $1 billion, can MCC really serve as an alternative to China's large quantities of foreign aid?

Answer. Yes it can. Because of the above limitations in the Chinese aid program, many countries prefer USAID or MCC aid help even though the MCC cannot compare to the size of the Chinese aid programs.

Question 3. Mr. Natsios, in your testimony you point out that we over-rely on numbers and figures to evaluate development success.

♦ Can you elaborate on this point?

Answer. My essay ("Clash of the Counter-Bureaucracy and Development") (see: http://www.cgdev.org/sites/default/files/1424271—file—Natsios—Counterbureaucracy.pdfdescribed) in the first answer goes into the problems with quantitative measurement in aid programming. I mentioned a book called Poor Numbers by Morten Jerven during the hearing which offers a scholarly (rather dry) analysis of the misuse of numbers in measuring economic growth in Africa.

♦ Shouldn't we estimate and measure our success in foreign aid?

Answer. In the old USAID we had an office called CDIE (the Center for Development Information and Evaluation) which used impact evaluations to analysis aid programs which used to be to gold standard in determining aid success internationally. If CDIE said something was working other donors and international organizations change their approach. Over the years the office became less effective because it was not staffed or funded properly. It used field based survey across countries to interview people at the local level to see if aid programs were successful or not.

Question 4. You also state in your written testimony that the entire system of aid oversight needs reform.

♦ What are your suggestions?

Answer. The last section of the essay "The Clash of the Counter-Bureaucracy and Development" proposed a series of regulatory reforms.

Question 5. Mr. Natsios, you mention in your written testimony that since MCC was created, we've expanded the list of indicators for country qualification for MCC from 17 indicators to 20.

♦ Are we overwhelming these developing countries with too many targets?

Answer. The more MCC, White House, or Congress increases the number of indicators the less affect each will have as poor countries do not have the institutional or organizational capacity to make that many changes to satisfy the demand for reform from donor governments. Few is better. As I indicated in my testimony the corruption indicator based on empirical evidence needs to be changed since it is the most important indicator statutorily. However I don't know many Senators and Congressmen who are going to vote to change the corruption indicator even if it is imprecise. The rule of law is a much better indicator, so perhaps the Committee could consider combining a rule of law indicator with the existing corruption indictor. That would help.

♦ Can you talk about which indicators should be prioritized the most?

Answer. The key to development is democracy and improved governance (done properly over the long term) and the right policies which encourage investment and trains and supports entrepreneurship. There are earmarks in the aid budget for the U.S. government for everything under the sun, except for democracy and governance programs and economic growth (they don't have a lot of support in Washington and they take too long to show results). What distinguishes highly advanced countries from those which are poor and dysfunctional are the productivity, density, legitimacy, and resilience of institutions-public, private, and non-profit.

♦ In your view, does adding additional indicators hurt a prospective MCC country's ability to focus their efforts?

Answer. More indicators will weaken the program. It is better to strengthen existing indicators or to update them, but not increase them.

Question 6. In the hearing, you briefly discussed the three types of aid programs: performance-based, need-based, and national interest-based. Would you elaborate on which programs you think are best suited for different types of aid needs? Which type of program would you suggest for aid programs in Africa? Would those differ than your suggestions for aid in South America or Eastern Europe?

Answer. I am writing a book on foreign aid and have created a framework for thinking about the distribution formulas for all of our aid programs. These distinctions I mentioned at the hearing are part of that framework, but only part. The USG also distributes aid to countries and through sectors based on (1) "future risk" and (2) on funding levels of aid in the previous year which I call the "inertial formula option." Generally global health programs and humanitarian response funding for programs to keep people alive in war zones, famines, and natural disasters should be need-based because by their nature they mean life or death for millions of people. The inertial distribution option is used when the disruption of existing programs would take place if money was constantly be moved around for other reasons. Determining national interest is not easily made and we generally leave that to the State Dept. and Congress to determine as it is a rather ambiguous term and funding levels are often a function of negotiation between the recipient country which we wish to influence or support and the State or Defense Dept. The MCC, agriculture programs, economic growth programs, and democracy and governance programs should be performance-based because their success is determined by the political will and past performance of the recipient country itself.

Question 7. You also mentioned aid funds coming out of the Economic Support Fund (ESF), specifically for interested-based and strategic aid programs.

♦ Would you elaborate on the decision-making process used to determine that funds should be pulled from that account?

Answer. During the Cold War the State Department had control over the programming of ESF funding in countries where the USG had critical national interests narrowly defined. Our aid programs in Egypt, Israel, and Jordan, for example were and still are paid for from that account. The State Dept. would transfer the funds to USAID with guidance as to which country should get how much money and set broad goals for the use of the funds. USAID controlled the Development Assistance Account, the Global Health Account, and Disaster Relief (IDA account). That discipline was lost so that now State effectively controls all of the accounts with the F reorganization of aid and is intimately involved from Washington and from the Embassies in how program decisions are made. Secretary Rice's reorganization of aid programming in 2006 and 2007 centralized aid funding decisions in the State Dept., but made the USAID Administrator dual-hatted so he or she would also serve as the Deputy Secretary of State for Foreign Assistance (a new position). That meant the USAID Administrator controlled both USAID funding and State Dept. aid programs. In 2009 Secretary Clinton separated the two positions-the USAID Administrator was no longer dual-hatted and lost control of both the USAID budget and programs and State Dept. aid programs. Effectively the State Dept. now controls all aid programming.

♦ Why do interest-based aid programs now use International Disaster Assistance (IDA) or Development Assistance (DA) funds rather than ESF funds?

Answer. When the President or Secretary of State makes an announcement of a new program or pledges USG funds at an international pledging conference State Dept. and OMB searches for ways to fund these new programs with existing resources since getting money for aid budgets in an era of fiscal restraint (the Executive Branch has not proposed a new federal budget in how many years?) they look to USAID budget to get the money by shutting down existing programs. When the USG faces a crisis such as the civil wars in Syria or Iraq the State Dept. tries to find funding from existing accounts, once again they shut down aid programs to do that.

In the old, more independent, USAID aid program during the Cold War programs typically lasted 10 to 20 years (which is how long it takes to create functioning institutions). The Green Revolution in Asia, one of the most successful aid programs of the 20th century that helped us win the Cold War and save at least 300 million lives (some say a billion lives) took thirty years to implement. The construction of 12 Engineering Schools in India linked with 12 of the best Engineering Schools in the U.S. was a 20 year USAID (and its predecessors) program (1951–1971). The high tech revolution in India today is based in those Indian Engineering Schools. It took 20 years to build them and strengthen them to be what they later became. Many USAID officers have told me that now all programs are reviewed each year since the State Dept. took control of the program and if they don't show immediate short term results funding is shut down and transferred to other more pressing needs. Evidence from political science research shows that new democracies require at least (and often more) 12–16 years to take root and mature. They cannot show sustainable results in three, four or five years.

♦ Can you speak to the pros and cons of each of these different funding streams?

Answer. The DA account was supposed to be for long term programs, while the ESF was for short term programs. The distinction does not hold much weight any longer.

Question 8. You alluded to an example where several mission directors, with their ambassadors, affirmatively tried to stop a compact because their country so obviously didn't qualify, and yet, were being considered to become candidate countries.

♦ Could you relay more information on this instance to me (if necessary, in a private letter)?

Answer I will provide the information to you privately.

♦ To what extent does the MCC board interact with USAID country mission directors? With U.S. ambassadors?

Answer. While I was in office there was little interaction between either the MCC board or the staff and USAID or the Embassies as Washington put out a cable which prohibited us from working with the country governments on the MCC programs. In practice we ignored the cable and helped design some of the MCC country programs because the countries themselves had no idea how to do it. Now I am told there is much more interaction between USAID and the MCC, especially when State tries to interfere in program management (particularly in the threshold programs) which neither USAID nor MCC likes. It does confuse officials in the developing countries to have a MCC Mission Director and a USAID Mission Director. More broadly the diffusion of USG aid programs abroad is rather chaotic since the different U.S. agencies and federal departments don't always give the same advice (sometimes they contradict each other).

♦ In your opinion, should there be more interaction between these parties or less?

Answer. More not less.

RESPONSE TO ADDITIONAL QUESTIONS FOR THE RECORD SUBMITTED TO DR. NANCY BIRDSALL BY MEMBERS OF THE COMMITTEE

Dr. Birdsall's Response to Senator Corker

Question 1. To date, the MCC Board has approved second compacts for six countries. Second compacts should require more selectivity than justpassing the indicators required in a first compact. In addition, one could certainly argue that with respect to whether a second compactwill be granted, the candidate country should be carefully judged on how well it has implemented the first compact.

♦ Do you agree with this view? What additional standards would you recommend be considered before granting a second compact?

Answer. Countries should be judged on implementation of their first compact, but second compacts should not "require more selectivity" for two reasons: (1) poverty-reducing growth is vulnerable to global external conditions and seldom takes a steady, simple path and (2) the scorecard is not a perfect measure of policy performance. Further, it is extremely difficult to pass the scorecard consistently over a period of seven or more years, from the time that a country is first selected to when it would be under consideration for a second compact. Only one country, Lesotho, has passed the scorecard every year since 2004.

In addition to the scorecard, it also makes sense for a country to be judged on the quality of the partnership during its first compact, including whether the partner country government was committed to undertaking agreed-upon reforms and worked to implement the compact expeditiously. MCC should be able to make these qualitative judgments but should be clear about when a country excluded from second compact consideration because of weak first compact implementation could be reconsidered. There may be compelling reasons, such as a change in government, why a country that was not a strong partner during a first compact could be considered for a second compact in the future.

MCC also looks for countries to exhibit positive "trends" on the corruption and democracy hurdles when under consideration for a second compact. However, I believe the agency should exercise caution and not weigh these "trends" too heavily, especially with respect to the corruption indicator. Changes in a given country's Control of Corruption score over a period of a few years are almost always small and well within the wide margins of error. Such small changes do not reflect substantive shifts in climate or policy.

♦ Do you think that second compacts should be required to address development issues above and beyond what is addressed in a first compact? What development challenges should second compacts address?

Answer. The focus of any compact should reflect the priorities of the partner country government, as informed by the constraints-to-growth analysis and other economic analysis that helps the two parties select projects most likely to achieve results. Second compacts might seek further progress in a sector addressed in a first compact if that sector remains a constraint to growth and has funding needs that are a good match for MCC investments. In other cases, it could make sense for a subsequent compact to focus on a different sector(s).

Question 2. The MCC indicators are an indispensable part of MCC's operations. However, the indicators are only as good as the data available and the specific models and statistics used to evaluate a candidate country's success in meeting the indicator goals.

♦ Are the current data sets and models adequate and appropriate and effective? What changes to the indicators or the date used to support evaluations do you recommend?

Answer. The data MCC uses are not perfect proxies of a country's policy performance, but such indicators don't exist. What's important is that the agency retains flexibility in how it interprets imprecise data. Therefore, while the best approach would be for MCC to remove the hard hurdle from the Control of Corruption indicator entirely, a second best approach would be to maintain the hard hurdle for initial selection (i.e. the first time a country is selected for a compact) but remove the stringency for reselections i.e., during the period of compact development. MCC should continue to monitor the partner country's policy performance, but no single indicator will do this job sufficiently once a partnership has started. While no statutory change is required to enable MCC to make this change, the agency will need support from members of Congress and other stakeholders in promoting the responsible use of data. Rather than focusing on whether or not the agency observes its hard hurdle rules to the letter, Congress can encourage MCC's board to engage in a nuanced dialogue about policy performance and help ensure that eligibility decisions are made based on actual governance quality rather than mere data noise.

That said, the agency should continue to look for better indicators as data sources change. MCC has been exploring options for alternative indicators and methodologies, especially alternative governance indicators. One new initiative that may help is the Governance Data Alliance, a group of civil society, private sector, and donor data producers, users, and funders committed to attaining more effective production and use of governance data. (MCC helped convene the initial group.)

I recommend Congress request a report every two years from MCC that outlines the agency's efforts to seek alternative sources of data. Among the factors the agency must consider when determining appropriate indicators are country coverage, regular periodicity, public availability from a third-party source, and broad enough applicability for most countries. To illustrate the last point, membership in the Extractive Industries Transparency Initiative, while important, is more applicable to some countries than others. Beyond those basic criteria, another characteristic of interest could be a greater focus on outcomes (e.g., percentage of electricity generated that is paid for, percent of vaccines delivered vs. paid for).

Question 3. In the hearing, you mentioned that there are many countries that may have pockets of wealth but also pockets of extreme poverty. There may countries that are badly governed but with pockets of well-governed regions within the country.

♦ What are your views on sub-national compacts? For example, should MCC be allowed to grant a sub-national compact if the economic rates of return are good and the local or regional entity receiving the compact is well-governed, even though the nation as a whole may not pass the MCC test either on the indica- tors at a national level or because the country is "too rich" at the national level?

Answer. In some cases sub-national compacts could make sense. Changing the definition of candidacy—to include countries with median consumption below $10 per day, for instance—would set the stage well for sub-national compacts in certain countries that have large pockets of poverty. Sub-national or geographically focused compacts in these countries could make sense.

However, the logic of a sub-national investment depends on the sector. Investing sub-nationally in a sector in which the national government can intervene may not make sense. For example, a sub-national compact relating to municipal water and sanitation using an outcomes-based aid approach might make sense so long as the central government has no ability to limit tariffs.

♦ What are the dangers or problems with such an approach?

Answer. There are some practical questions and considerations about how   the agency might pursue sub-national compacts:[1]

> *How would MCC pick sub-national regions?* MCC has long stressed the importance of using high-quality, transparent, and broadly comparable third-party data to evaluate countries for eligibility. This type of information does not exist for sub-national units within most developing countries-and certainly not for sub-national units across countries. This is less of a restriction for countries that pass the (national-level) scorecard. In those cases, MCC could plausibly work with sub-national units that express interest. However, to the extent that MCC might work in well-governed pockets of countries that do not pass the national-level scorecards, selecting where to work in a transparent, comparative way would be more difficult. For example, neither Nigeria nor Kenya pass the scorecard but could have relatively well-governed sub-national units. However, it would be hard for MCC to systematically and impartially compare policy performance among 36 Nigerian states. Comparing the performance of these states to counties in Kenya-or to sub-national units in countries that do pass the scorecard-could be even more complex.

> *Sectors are limited.* MCC compacts are all accompanied by certain policy and regulatory changes that the partner government agrees to undertake. The success of MCC's investment is contingent upon the partner government's contribution in these areas. Because of this, it would be important for sub-national compacts to focus in sectors in which the sub-national government has jurisdiction and the national government is uninvolved.

Question 4. There appears to be a growing trend whereby certain countries have been cracking down on international civil society NGO's through politically motivated investigations or registration laws. These actions appear designed to chill the activities of these civil society groups or drive them out altogether. It would be inappropriate to provide a compact to a candidate country that is unduly persecuting civil society.

♦ Should Congress consider adjusting the indicators to include an evaluation of the enabling environment for civil society in a candidate country?

Answer. There is no need to do so. The current democracy hard hurdle requires countries to pass either the Political Rights or Civil Liberties indicators. In practice, most countries that pass one also pass the other. In FY 2016, 74 out of 81 MCC candidate countries (91%) either pass both or fail both. The current Civil Liberties indicator includes an assessment of freedom for nongovernmental organizations. However, MCC should be open to changes to the indicators should better ones emerge. For the agency to be able to make such changes it is important that its flexibility to do so be preserved.

♦ Should the MCC develop internal reporting requirements so that the MCC Board, before approving a country compact, is fully informed and in a position to evaluate whether the candidate country has been taking actions intended to discriminate and discourage civil society groups from engaging in legitimate democratic development?

Answer. This would be a reasonable piece of supplemental information for MCC to provide its board before asking it to make a decision about compact eligibility or compact approval.

ADDENDUM

(1) As I indicated during my testimony, I wanted to provide additional details on the history of country selection without complete fidelity to the scorecard and to the scorecard-related challenges faced by countries who suddenly graduate to a new income category.

Only two countries have ever been newly selected for compact eligibility despite not passing MCC's scorecard. This happened with Georgia on two occasions and with Mozambique once. Georgia and Mozambique were each among the initial tranche of countries selected for MCC compact eligibility in May 2004. In both cases, MCC was aware of substantial reform efforts that had taken place in the months since the data reflected on the scorecard were collected, and the agency was con-

---

[1] Rose, Sarah. 2014. Regional and Sub-National Compact Considerations for the Millennium Challenge Corporation. Washington, DC: Center for Global Development. http://www.cgdev.org/publication/regional-and-sub-national-compact-considerations-millennium-challenge-corporation

vinced that both countries would fully meet the scorecard criteria in the near future. On this count the agency was right-Georgia passed by 2007, Mozambique by 2006. Since the agency's first selection round in 2004, MCC has been more inclined to wait until existing reform efforts are reflected in the scorecard's indicators before selecting a country. The only exception has been Georgia again, which was selected in FY11 for a second compact despite not passing the scorecard. In this case, the country fell short by one indicator in the "Investing in People" category, but the data did not reflect significant policy concerns. Specifically, the Immunization Rates indicator was affected by a temporary shortage of a vaccine but was expected to rebound the following year.

While MCC certainly faces political pressures, the agency's record on country eligibility overwhelmingly suggests the prioritization of policy performance over politics as the main and necessary criterion for selection. (2) During my testimony, I also noted that countries (for example, Moldova) occasionally have not been considered for second compacts because they graduate to lower middle income and no longer pass the corruption hurdle in this tougher group, though there is not evidence of a substantial deterioration in performance. The broader point here is that the hard hurdle on corruption can lead to decisions that make little sense for development. MCC should be able to select for a second compact those countries that have demonstrated good partnership during the first compact and have not had a meaningful policy deterioration. A just-below-the-median score on an imprecise indicator and/or graduation to the lower middle income category do not reflect such a change.

(2)During my testimony, I also noted that countries (for example, Moldova) occasionally have not been considered for second compacts because they graduate to lower middle income and no longer pass the corruption hurdle in this tougher group, though there is not evidence of a substantial deterioration in performance. The broader point here is that the hard hurdle on corruption can lead to decisions that make little sense for development. MCC should be able to select for a second compact those countries that have demonstrated good partnership during the first compact and have not had a meaningful policy deterioration. A just-below-the-median score on an imprecise indicator and/or graduation to the lower middle income category do not reflect such a change.

Dr. Birdsall's Response to Senator Cardin

Question 1. In your testimony you highlighted the need for a better definition of poverty for country candidacy. How would you envision MCC operating in countries that currently exceed MCC's GNI per capita ceiling, but still have widespread poverty? Which metric do you feel best captures poverty for MCC's purposes?

Answer. Median consumption is a promising choice. The indicator is a better reflection of people's well-being because it excludes government spending (on defense, for example) and public and private investment except as they affect household income; and because unlike the average or mean measure, it corrects for the skewness in the income distribution of virtually all countries, and thus reflects well typical individual material well-being in a country.[1] While median consumption is not available for every country, the agency could sidestep any gaps in data by layering median consumption on top of the current GNI per capita measure. Countries that fall below either threshold—it might be $10 a day for median consumption and it's currently $4,125 GNI per capita—would comprise the potential candidate pool.

Question 2. The MCC legislative mandate is to lessen poverty through economic growth. In your view, are sufficient funds being provided to each country to make a significant difference in their poverty levels?

Answer. The fundamental question here is whether MCC support, in the form of funding but also through dialogue and negotiation, reinforces good policies in a country. Ultimately, it is the countries' policies that really matter when it comes to spurring poverty-reducing growth.

Question 3. What are your recommendations for reforming the control of corruption indicator? In your view, what is the best way to measure and hold countries

[1] Birdsall, Nancy and Christian Meyer. 2014. The Median Is the Message: A Good-Enough Measure of Material Well-Being and Shared Development Progress. Washington, DC: Center for Global Development. http://www.cgdev.org/publication/median-message-good-enough-measure-material-well-being-and-shared-development-progress

accountable for tackling corruption while simultaneously providing MCC the flexibility to interpret data in the context of on-the-ground realities?

Answer. MCC's authorizing legislation outlines the kinds of policy areas the agency should consider when making eligibility determinations, but it does not specify which indicators should be used, nor does it describe how they should be interpreted. As a result, the agency has both good guidance and necessary flexibility in choosing and interpreting indicators. The agency needs support from Congress to utilize this combination in a way that reflects on-the-ground realities, while resisting what are sometimes short-term pressures from political and advocacy groups.

Unfortunately, all existing composite measures and indices lack an objective basis. Research conducted by the Center for Global Development, Hating on the Hurdle and Focus on Policy Performance: MCC's Model in Practice explain in detail the current Control of Corruption indicator's limitations and why using it as a "hard hurdle" that countries are required to pass is problematic.[2]

It is especially problematic for decisions around continuing partnerships. There's some justification for using Control of Corruption as a hard hurdle for initial selection into MCC eligibility because it provides a transparent basis for those decisions. However, once selected to begin a partnership, countries must be reselected each year while developing a compact, a process that usually takes 2-3 years. Applying the hard hurdle to countries during this stage does not make sense since countries can move from passing to failing for non-substantive reasons like small score movements within the margin of error or shifting from the low income group to the more competitive lower middle income group. Curtailing an ongoing relationship with a country that has had no real deterioration in policy performance because of its score on an imprecise indicator threatens MCC's credibility as a reasonable and rational development partner.

Therefore, while the best approach would be for MCC to remove the hard hurdle from the Control of Corruption indicator entirely, a second best approach would be to maintain the hard hurdle for initial selection (i.e. the first time a country is selected for a compact) but remove the stringency for reselections i.e., during the period of compact development. MCC should continue to monitor the partner country's policy performance, but no single indicator will do this job sufficiently once a partnership has started.

See response to question 4e on other ways to measure corruption.

Question. In his written testimony, Mr. Natsios suggested that given the limitations of the underlying data behind the control of corruption indicator, the hard hurdle for candidate countries should be replaced with the rule of law indicator.

a. How does the data quality between these two indicators compare?

Answer. The Control of Corruption indicator and the Rule of Law indicator are part of the same Worldwide Governance Indicators series, produced by the World Bank Institute and Brookings Institution. The aggregation methodology is the same, as are many of the underlying sources, so the quality of the two measures should be considered essentially the same.

b. How quickly does each indicator respond to policy reforms or other on-the-ground changes?

Answer. Neither indicator is particularly actionable. This is due, in part, to the breadth of topics each one covers. Rule of law, for instance, measures the extent of violent and organized crime, trust in police, contract enforceability, the independence and efficiency of the judicial process, private property protection, and intellectual property rights protection. Even substantial reform in one of these areas may not have an outsized effect on the indicator because it encompasses so many components.

The indicators also measure things that are slow to change in a meaningful, institutionalized way. Further, I would caution that highly-responsive measures of corruption or rule of law may not be particularly desirable. For instance, it would not necessarily be helpful for a country to see a markedly improved score upon the establishment of an anti-corruption commission when it then takes years to assess whether or not it will be an effective, funded, and permanent institution.

[2] Dunning, Casey, Jonathan Karver, and Charles Kenny. 2014. Hating on the Hurdle: Reforming the Millennium Challenge Corporation's Approach to Corruption. Washington, DC: Center for Global Development. http://www.cgdev.org/publication/hating-hurdle-reforming-millennium-challenge-corporations-approach-corruption Rose, Sarah and Franck Wiebe. 2015. Focus on Policy Performance: MCC's Model in Practice. Washington, DC: Center for Global Development. http://www.cgdev.org/publication/focus-policy-performance-mccs-model-practice

There was concern expressed at the hearing that because the Control of Corruption indicator measures perceptions it can be easily influenced by "marketing" or campaigning by the government. However, since the indicator aggregates a number of different types of perceptions·up to around 20 sources of expert assessments, firm-level surveys, and citizen-level surveys·the data are not particularly sensitive to that kind of activity. This aggregation is a useful characteristic, but it is another reason why the data are slow to move·the perceptions of many, both inside and outside the country, are unlikely to turn on a dime.

    c. Is simply swapping one indicator for another in this sense the best way to incentivize potential candidate countries to tackle corruption?

Answer. Ultimately, this indicator's purpose is less about incentivizing anti-corruption measures and more about avoiding putting money into countries that will not use it well. No amount of outside funding is likely to influence whether or not a government "chooses" corruption. In fact, a study by AidData and the College of William and Mary found that, in general, donors' or international non-governmental organizations' "scorecards," rankings, and other policy assessments that focus on countries' political governance have little influence over countries' policy choices.[3]

    d. Do you feel making this statutory change would preserve the intent of provi·sion while simultaneously allowing MCC sufficient flexibility to balance the indicator score with the sometimes conflicting realities that are observed on the ground?

Answer. It is extremely important for MCC to have the flexibility to balance scores with sometimes conflicting realities.

The statute does not mandate the corruption indicator serve as a hard hurdle, so no statutory changes are necessary to ensure the agency maintains this flexibility. But members of Congress and other stakeholders can help by promoting responsible use of data by MCC and its board. Rather than focusing on whether or not the agency observes its hard hurdle rules to the letter, stakeholders with an understanding of the strengths and weaknesses of the indicators can encourage MCC's board to engage in a nuanced dialogue about policy performance and help ensure that eligibility decisions are made based on actual governance quality rather than mere data noise.

    e. Have you identified alternative measures of corruption that could be adopted in place of the current metric, for example, Transparency International's Corruptions Perception Index? If so, what are the advantages and disadvantages of each?

Answer. No indicator is precise enough to act as a hard hurdle. The better ones are composites and are transparent about the standard errors of all components across countries (the current Control of Corruption indicator is one of these). Using a hard hurdle around the median for any corruption indicator is fraught, especially when many countries are concentrated around median, as is currently the case.

My understanding is that MCC has been exploring options for an alternative corruption indicator. One new initiative that may help is the Governance Data Alliance, a group of civil society, private sector, and donor data producers, users, and funders committed to attaining more effective production and use of governance data. (MCC helped convene the initial group.)

I recommend Congress request a report from MCC every two years that outlines the agency's efforts to seek alternative sources of data. Among the factors the agency must consider when determining appropriate indicators are country coverage, regular periodicity, public availability from a third-party source, and broad enough applicability for most countries. To illustrate the last point, something like membership in the Extractive Industries Transparency Initiative, while important, is more applicable to some countries than others. Beyond those basic criteria, another characteristic of interest could be a greater focus on outcomes (e.g., percentage of electricity generated that is paid for, percent of vaccines delivered vs. paid for).

    f. Would a hybrid of the control of corruption indicator and the rule of law indicator be practical and more informative for MCC's country selection?

Answer. Both are areas that merit measurement and inclusion on MCC's scorecard. But while a potential future indicator could combine some aspects of the two thematic areas, combining the two existing indicators would yield little benefit or additional information because the two are highly correlated. For the most recent year's data the correlation between the two indicators is 0.93 across all 215 coun-

[3] AidData and William & Mary Institute for the Theory & Practice of International Relations. 2015. The Marketplace of Ideas for Policy Change. Williamsburg: AidData. http://aiddata.org/marketplace-of-ideas-for-policy-change. See also, http://www.cgdev.org/blog/dive-new-data-mcc-effect.

tries and 0.83 for just the set of low and lower middle income countries MCC assesses.

    g. Would you recommend any statutory changes to allow more flexibility in the application of the control of corruption indicator?

Answer. The current statute provides flexibility in the interpretation of the control of corruption indicator. MCC specifies use of the hard hurdle in its annual selection methodology report. In the past, the agency has fallen under pressure from Congress and others to maintain strict observance of the hard hurdle interpretation. Congress should ask for regular reports on how MCC is measuring corruption (see 4e above), as an alternative to inappropriate "hard hurdle" approach.

    h. Would you support Mr. Natsios' suggestion to adopt the rule of law indicator   in place of the control of corruption indicator?

Answer. A measure of both rule of law and control of corruption have their place on MCC's scorecards. Neither should serve as a hard hurdle. Shifting the hurdle from Control of Corruption to Rule of Law would not eliminate the core problem of the indicator being too imprecise to warrant rigid interpretation.

ADDENDUM:

(1) As I indicated during my testimony, I wanted to provide additional details on the history of country selection without complete fidelity to the scorecard and to the scorecard-related challenges faced by countries who suddenly graduate to a new income category.

Only two countries have ever been newly selected for compact eligibility despite not passing MCC's scorecard. This happened with Georgia on two occasions and with Mozambique once. Georgia and Mozambique were each among the initial tranche of countries selected for MCC compact eligibility in May 2004. In both cases, MCC was aware of substantial reform efforts that had taken place in the months since the data reflected on the scorecard were collected, and the agency was convinced that both countries would fully meet the scorecard criteria in the near future. On this count the agency was right—Georgia passed by 2007, Mozambique by 2006. Since the agency's first selection round in 2004, MCC has been more inclined to wait until existing reform efforts are reflected in the scorecard's indicators before selecting a country. The only exception has been Georgia again, which was selected in FY11 for a second compact despite not passing the scorecard. In this case, the country fell short by one indicator in the "Investing in People" category, but the data did not reflect significant policy concerns. Specifically, the Immunization Rates indicator was affected by a temporary shortage of a vaccine but was expected to rebound the following year.

While MCC certainly faces political pressures, the agency's record on country eligibility overwhelmingly suggests the prioritization of policy performance over politics as the main and necessary criterion for selection.

(2) During my testimony, I also noted that countries (for example, Moldova) occasionally have not been considered for second compacts because they graduate to lower middle income and no longer pass the corruption hurdle in this tougher group, though there is not evidence of a substantial deterioration in performance. The broader point here is that the hard hurdle on corruption can lead to decisions that make little sense for development. MCC should be able to select for a second compact those countries that have demonstrated good partnership during the first compact and have not had a meaningful policy deterioration. A just-below-the-median score on an imprecise indicator and/or graduation to the lower middle income category do not reflect such a change.

MCC FY 16 Candidate Pool
(81 Countries)

Lower Income Countries (LICs)

- *Afghanistan*
- *Bangladesh*
- **Benin**
- **Burkina Faso**
- ~~*Burma*~~
- *Burundi*
- *Cambodia*
- *Cameroon*
- *CAR*
- *Chad*
- <u>*Comoros*</u>
- **Cote d'Ivoire**
- *Djibouti*
- ~~*Eritrea*~~
- *Ethiopia*
- *Gambia*
- **Ghana**
- *Guinea*
- *Guinea-Bissau*
- *Haiti*
- India
- Kenya
- *Kyrgyzstan*
- *Laos*
- **Lesotho**
- **Liberia**
- *Madagascar*
- **Malawi**
- *Mali*
- *Mauritania*
- **Mozambique**
- **Nepal**
- *Nicaragua*
- **Niger**
- ~~*North Korea*~~
- *Pakistan*
- *Rwanda*
- Sao Tome
- **Senegal**
- *Sierra Leone*
- <u>Solomon Islands</u>
- *Somalia*
- ~~South Sudan~~
- *Sudan*
- *Tajikistan*
- **Tanzania**
- *Togo*
- *Uganda*
- *Vietnam*
- *Yemen*
- **Zambia**
- ~~*Zimbabwe*~~

Lower Middle Income Countries (LMICs)

- Armenia
- <u>Bhutan</u>
- ~~Bolivia~~
- **Cabo Verde**
- *Congo-B*
- *Egypt*
- **El Salvador**
- **Georgia**
- *Guatemala*
- *Guyana*
- *Honduras*
- *Indonesia*
- <u>Kiribati</u>
- **Kosovo**
- *Micronesia*
- *Moldova*
- **Morocco**
- *Nigeria*
- *Papua NG*
- **Philippines**
- <u>Samoa</u>
- *Sri Lanka*
- *Swaziland*
- ~~Syria~~
- *Timor-Leste*
- *Ukraine*
- *Uzbekistan*
- <u>Vanuatu</u>

8 countries in red are statutorily prohibited from MCC

44 of the remaining 73 countries in blue *Italic* did not pass the FY16 scorecard

14 countries in bold are current MCC countries

<u>7 small population states</u>

Examples of countries prohibited from MCC Funds due to UMIC status:
Paraguay ($4150 GNI/capita)
Belize ($4510)
Jamaica ($5220)
Dom Rep ($5950)
Ecuador ($6040)
Peru ($6410)

*Using the WB's LIC ($0-$1985 GNI/capita) and LMIC ($1986-$4125 GNI/capita) definitions. By law, the candidate pool does not include UMIC countries

www.ingramcontent.com/pod-product-compliance
Lightning Source LLC
Chambersburg PA
CBHW081403280526
45788CB00009B/2974